The Methuen Drama Book of
Modern Monologues
for Women

Edited by
CHRYS SALT

Methuen Drama

Methuen Drama

10 9 8 7 6 5 4 3

Methuen Drama
A & C Black Publishers Ltd
36 Soho Square,
London W1D 3QY

Copyright in this selection © by Chrys Salt 2004

A CIP catalogue record for this book is available from the British Library

ISBN 978 0 413 77424 8

Typeset by SX Composing DTP, Rayleigh, Essex
Printed and bound in Great Britain by
CPI Cox and Wyman, Reading, Berkshire

Disclaimer

Methuen Drama gratefully acknowledges the permissions granted
to reproduce the quoted extracts within this work. Every effort has been made to
trace the current copyright holders of the extracts included in this work. The
publishers apologise for any unintended omissions and would be pleased to
receive any information that would enable them to amend any inaccuracies or
omissions in future editions.

Contents

Introduction

This selection of monologues is drawn from plays written between the second half of the nineteenth century (Wedekind, Wilde, Hauptmann, Jarry) to the 1970s (Dario Fo, Ayckbourn, Gems, Duras), stopping off along the way to visit many of the playwrights who helped to fashion modern theatre. I have chosen pieces that offer challenges to your skill and imagination, and have tried to introduce as much variety as possible in terms of character, age, style and content.

My aim has been to direct you towards audition pieces that are not only *right* for you, but *right* for the audition in hand, so you can bring your unique qualities as an artist to the character you have chosen.

When you are called to audition, you will either be asked to read a chunk of text 'cold', as in 'She's a Lithuanian pole vaulter with a penchant for beer . . . would you mind reading it for me?', or you will be asked to perform something from your audition repertoire. You'll certainly need a handful of pieces under your belt whether it's the usual 'one classical and one contemporary piece' for drama school entry or something prepared for a specific audition for a theatre, a fringe company or even an agent.

In any event, it's valuable experience to research a play and perform a speech – even if it has no immediate purpose. It keeps your mind alive and your creative juices flowing.

When you are choosing your audition pieces, think carefully what suits you and what you are auditioning for. No good wheeling out your deathless Antigone for Theatre in Education (TIE) or that Victoria Wood monologue for the latest Gary Mitchell play. Nor should you render your Juliet if you are fully forty-two and look like an escapee from *East Enders*. Be sensible. It's horses for courses isn't it?

When I was writing my book, *Make Acting Work*, I had an interesting chat with Jude Kelly (former Artistic Director of the West Yorkshire Playhouse). I'll quote it again because you might like to bear what she says in mind when deciding which piece to choose.

It's very hard to make actors understand that you are often not turning them down because they are less good than somebody else – you turn them down because they are not . . . right in some way. Actors get very upset about this and yet if you ask them what they think of such and such a production, they often say 'So and so was completely wrong for that part'. At the same time they will be arguing for a completely level playing field without any version of 'typecasting' at all . . . .

Your task at audition is not only to show that you might be right for *this particular job*, but that you are an artist with talent and imagination – so even if you are not 'right' this time round you will certainly stick in my mind when I am casting a similar role again. Remember casting personnel probably don't have a file for 'good actor'. How could they keep track? But they might have one for 'glamorous granny', 'sexy blonde' or 'tough professional'. They'll want to keep you on file if your work has impressed.

Some parts fit like thermal underpants. They are comfortable, snug. They belong to you. Something inside you keys into the character's soul. The feelings she expresses, the language she uses. Her class. Her agenda. Her emotional equipment. It just feels 'right' The text comes 'trippingly off the tongue'. You have the right physical equipment. These are the pieces to go for. You may be wearing them for some time, so make sure they fit.

An audition piece should be a little artefact in its own right. Sometimes (heresy oh heresy) you won't need to read the play. Taken out of context you can make it your own. I recently snaffled a piece from an old Emlyn Williams play *The Corn is Green* (set in Welsh mining community). Out of context, with a bit of tinkering and an alternative 'back story', it worked well for an Irish actor with a line in IRA terrorists. (Sorry Emlyn!)

On most occasions, however, it's *vital* to read the play. And don't read it once, read it several times. There's an apocryphal story about the actor who goes into the radio studio to read *A Book at Bedtime*. He hasn't read the book and thinks he can wing it. It is only when he gets deep into Chapter 1 and reads 'said Stephen with his customary lisp' . . . He hadn't done his homework, so do yours.

A couple of minutes is a short space of time for you to 'strut your stuff', so here are a few tips I hope you will find helpful. Bear them in mind in conjunction with the commentaries I have written when you are doing your study.

- Find out every last thing you can about your character and her journey. Look at the writer's stage directions. They will give you valuable clues. What do other people have to say about her? What has happened to her? What drives her? What does she want? Where has she come from? Where is she now? Church? Park? Drawing room? Arctic waste? Sauna? Who is she talking to? What's their relationship? Why is she saying this now? What is the style? What's the period? What does she do for a living? What's she wearing? Crinoline? Stilettos? Trainers? Everything makes a difference! It's 1902. Did women cross their legs? Rigour is the name of the game! Play the situation. Play the intention. The text is just the icing on the cake. If I say 'You have lovely blue eyes', am I making an observation, admiring your physical attributes or telling you I love you? How many other things could it mean? Try it using a different subtext each time. You'll see what I mean.
- Never watch yourself in the mirror or listen to yourself on tape. You'll end up trying to reproduce that magic gesture, that meaningful inflection. Unless you engage with the character afresh each time, your audition piece will become a stilted, stale affair – all form and no content.
- Practice your pieces regularly so you are not caught on the hop when the phone rings.
- Don't let nerves carry you off. Fear is the enemy and will spoil all that beautiful work you did in the bedroom. If you don't get this job, you won't lose a leg. Get your audition in perspective. Remember, if I've asked to see you, I *want* you to be good. It would be such a relief to cast this part, fill this course or take you on as a client. Do me a favour and give yourself a chance. Take

some time before you begin. Close your eyes for a few moments. I'm happy to wait for your good work. Breathe deeply. Engage with your character. Exclude the paraphernalia of the audition situation from your thinking. You are no longer in a cluttered office at Television Centre or facing a battalion of watchful faces. You are in nineteenth-century France! Or facing the child you gave away twenty years ago. You are not here to show how clever you are. You are not *showing*, you are *being*. You are here to bring two minutes of your character's breathing life into my room. The ground under your feet is the ground she walks! You have slipped into her skin. You wear her life. You have transformed.

- Wear something you feel comfortable in. Those biting new shoes will distract you from the job in hand. Dress appropriately. Foolish to wear your décolletage for that solicitor, or those stilettos for Lady Anne.
- Keep your hair out of your face. I need to see your eyes. They really are the mirrors of the soul. If you are *thinking* it right, it will *be* right. It won't matter to me how brilliantly you can mime drowning in a vat of porridge, if your work doesn't have the ring of truth about it, I won't be interested.

So it's over to you. My commentaries should not be seen as 'giving direction' in anything but the loosest sense. But I have tried to give a few tips and indicators about the acting style, context, interpretation and approach, and point you towards a few clues buried in the language or the syntax. They are by no means intended to be definitive – how could they be? – but I hope they will help when you are doing your own researches.

The pieces are arranged in an 'age ladder' with the youngsters at the beginning, so I hope that will make it easy for you to locate an appropriate piece. Sometimes of course a character's age is flexible and can be adapted to work for you so I have avoided being too specific. I have left in stage directions where they seem relevant and, on the odd occasion, slightly tinkered with the text (where indicated) so it works better out of context. I hope you will find this useful.

May the creative force be with you. Good luck.

This book is dedicated to Nina Finburgh, with love and thanks.

Thanks to my students and all my friends and colleagues in the business. To Elizabeth Ingrams who as editor at Methuen was patience itself over a difficult year and to Mark Dudgeon, my current editor, for invaluable help with this collection.

Miss Julie *by August Strindberg*
(translated by Michael Meyer)

Strindberg is seen by many as the father of twentieth-century theatre. He sought to break the mould of the 'stagy' classical tradition of the nineteenth century, demanding a more naturalistic approach from his actors. He describes *Miss Julie* as 'the first in a series of naturalistic tragedies', and the dialogue does feel startlingly contemporary.

The play is set on the night of a midsummer party in a large manor house belonging to Miss Julie's father. Excited by the dancing, Miss Julie makes for the kitchen where she finds her father's footman, Jean, and the man's fiancée, Christine. Jean is handsome, arrogant and self-educated, with ideas above his station. Miss Julie is young, aristocratic, feisty, incendiary, coquettish, and manipulative. She delights in flouting the rules of her sex and class. There is a sizzling sexual attraction between them that provides the basic ingredient for a drama in which a cat and mouse, love-hate game of sexual and class politics is played out.

Jean is 'inflammable material', and Miss Julie relishes playing with fire. While Christine sleeps, Miss Julie allows Jean to seduce her. Confronting the situation in the cold light of morning, Miss Julie demands Jean runs away with her to avoid disgrace and she steals money from her father to fund their escape. Just prior to this speech, Jean has brutally decapitated her pet greenfinch with a kitchen axe, rather than allow her to take it with her.

This is a difficult monologue to approach as it starts at full emotional throttle. Take time to engage with her fury before you begin. Imagine Miss Julie's situation. Her lover has just killed her pet. She is pre-menstrual. She has been brought up by her mother to believe a woman can be just as good as a man; to distrust and despise them, and not to be any man's slave. But Jean is one man she cannot master. She can't 'pull rank' because she has demeaned herself by being 'too easy'.

She snarls and hisses like a caged animal, desperately trying to hang on to her shredded status, summoning the most bloodthirsty language, painting the most degrading scenarios with the most unlikely outcomes. Even when she hears her father's carriage return, she delays departure flying dangerously close to the flame. But nothing touches Jean. He watches implacably, stoking her rage with his indifference. There is no way out for Miss Julie. If she leaves with Jean, she ties herself to a servant and a man whom she loathes. If she stays, she risks discovery and shame.

The slaughter of the greenfinch is a defining moment in the play. It triggers this man-hating, class-ridden tirade and signals a bloody and fatal outcome.

Miss Julie (*screams*) Kill me too! Kill me! You, who can slaughter an innocent creature without a tremor! Oh, I hate and detest you! There is blood between us now! I curse the moment I set eyes on you, I curse the moment I was conceived in my mother's womb!

[Jean What's the good of cursing? Come!]

Miss Julie (*goes towards the chopping block, as though drawn against her will*) No, I don't want to go yet. I can't – I must see – ssh! There's a carriage outside! (*She listens, but keeps her eyes fixed all the while on the chopping block and the axe.*) Do you think I can't bear the sight of blood? You think I'm so weak – oh, I should like to see your blood, your brains, on a chopping block – I'd like to see all your sex swimming in a lake of blood – I think I could drink from your skull, I'd like to bathe my feet in your guts, I could eat your heart, roasted! You think I'm weak – you think I loved you, because my womb wanted your seed, you think I want to carry your embryo under my heart and feed it with my blood, bear your child and take your name! By the way, what is your surname! I've never heard it – you probably haven't any. I'd have to be 'Mrs Kitchen-boy', or 'Mrs Lavatory man' – you dog, who wear my collar, you lackey who carry my crest on your buttons – am I to share with my own cook, compete with a scullery slut? Oh, oh, oh! You think I'm a coward and want to run away? No, now I shall stay. Let the storm break! My father will come home – find his desk broken open – his money gone! He'll ring – this bell – twice, for his lackey – then he'll send for the police – and I shall tell everything. Everything. Oh, it'll be good to end it all – if only it could be the end. And then he'll have a stroke and die. Then we shall all be finished, and there'll be peace – peace – eternal rest! And the coat of arms will be broken over the coffin – the title extinct – and the lackey's line will be carried on in an orphanage, win laurels in the gutter, and end in a prison!

Roots *by Arnold Wesker*

Roots is the middle play in Wesker's 'trilogy' written in the 1950s which begins with *Chicken Soup with Barley* and ends with *I'm Talking about Jerusalem*. Centring on over two decades in the lives of the Kahn family, it explores the battle between socialist ideals and economic and social reality.

Roots is a play about self-discovery and intellectual awakening set in rural Norfolk. Wesker has written the dialogue in the Norfolk dialect, which is essential to the poetry and cadence of the text.

Beatie is 'ample, blond and healthy-faced', the twenty-two-year-old daughter of poor Norfolk agricultural labourers who have little interest in anything beyond their limited lives. She has been working in London as a waitress since leaving school and has met and fallen in love with Ronnie Kahn, a Jewish self-educated chef who has attempted to inspire her with ideas about life, education and socialism. Although Beatie has been a resistant pupil, Ronnie's 'schooling' has filled her with ill-defined longings for another way of being. When she comes home for a visit, she vents her frustration on her family, disparaging their ignorance, blinkered views and inability to discuss things that matter. But the real target of her frustration is herself. Like them she has no real views of her own only being able to quote second hand opinions about politics, music and art that Ronnie has taught her.

At the end of the play the whole family have tried to put their differences behind them. They have gathered round a spread in their Sunday best for an impending visit from Beatie's fiancé. But at the eleventh hour, a letter comes from Ronnie telling Beatie that he doesn't think their relationship will work – doomed to failure by Beatie's inability to embrace his ideals. Beatie is distraught, but the family's reaction is a disgusted and unsupportive 'I told you so'. Stung into self-defence, Beatie launches into this speech which is the final one of the play. Instead of blaming Ronnie for his rejection, she turns on the family in an impassioned indictment of their narrow values, working class apathy, and a society that panders to it, despises it and profits from it. Suddenly Beatie is speaking for herself and instead of quoting Ronnie she finds herself expressing her own opinions about her life, her family and her class. She has finally found a voice, and as the speech gains momentum she grows more articulate and empowered. 'Blust' is Norfolk for 'Blast'. Look how Wesker uses it to propel the speech with extra explosive gusts of energy.

It is only at the end of the speech that Beatie pauses to realise what has happened to her – that at last she is speaking for herself and understands what Ronnie was trying to teach her. Her joy is almost transcendental as she embraces her 'awakened' self.

——————————————

Beatie Oh, *he* thinks we count alright – living in mystic communion with nature. Living in mystic bloody communion with nature (indeed). But us count? Count mother? I wonder. Do we? Do you think we really count? You don' wanna take any notice of what them ole papers say about the workers bein' all important these days – that's all squit! 'Cos we aren't. Do you think when the really talented people in the country get to work they get to work for us? Hell if they do! Do you think they don't know we 'ont make the effort? The writers don't write thinkin' we can understand, nor the painters don't paint expecting us to be interested – that they don't, nor don't the composers give out music thinking we can appreciate it. 'Blust,' they say, 'the masses is too stupid for us to come down to them. Blust,' they say, 'if they don't make no effort why should we bother?' So you know who come along? The slop singers and the pop writers and the film makers and women's magazines and the Sunday papers and the picture strip love stories – that's who come along, and you don't have to make no effort for them, it come easy. 'We know where the money lie,' they say, 'hell we do! The workers' ve got it so let's give them what they want. If they want slop songs and film idols we'll give 'em that then. If they want words of one syllable, we'll give 'em that then. If they want the third rate, BLUST! We'll give 'em THAT then. Anything's good enough for them 'cos they don't ask for no more!' The whole stinkin' commercial world insults us and we don't care a damn. Well, Ronnie's right – it's our own bloody fault. We want the third-rate – we got it! We got it! We got it! We . . .

Suddenly **Beatie** *stops as if listening to herself. She pauses, turns with an ecstatic smile on her face —*

D'you hear that? D'you hear it? Did you listen to me? I'm talking. Jenny, Frankie, mother – I'm not quoting no more.

The Springtime of Others *by Jean-Jacques Bernard (translated by John Leslie Frith)*

The Springtime of Others was first performed in Paris in 1924, then in English translation at the Everyman Theatre, Hampstead, in 1926. It is a delicate play about the relationship between mother and daughter when one is coming into bloom and the other's bloom is fading.

At the beginning, a young man nervously approaches Clarisse, a still beautiful Parisian widow in her forties. She reclines in the garden of an Italian hotel where she is on holiday with her eighteen-year-old daughter, Gilberte. She is mourning a failed relationship. Flattered by this much younger man's attentions, she misconstrues his intentions and flirtatiously encourages him. But when her daughter joins them, the reason for Maurice's presence is explained. He has come to ask for her Gilberte's hand in marriage. She realises she has been contesting with her daughter for the same man! Visibly thrown, she can say nothing.

Gilberte is a sensitive, loving young woman who misreads her mother's reaction, thinking she is upset at being kept in the dark. She is on emotional tenterhooks and at pains to explain why the time was never right to tell her. She is full of the excitement of young love, desperate to be given her mother's approval and avoid her anger. Gilberte cajoles, explains and apologises while her mother listens impassively, her eyes never leaving Gilberte's face.

Look at the punctuation. Gilberte always pre-empts her mother's questions and criticism, offering excuses and reasons for her secrecy before her mother can comment, determined to convince her that she has done nothing wrong! We get a sense of the kind of mother Clarisse has been by reading between the lines. Why is Gilberte so afraid to speak for instance? Consider what we learn from Gilberte's excuses: '. . . you've been so worried and unhappy', '. . . we're so seldom really alone together', 'You always had something else to do.' Look how she softens her mother up with childish endearments before tactfully criticising her for not treating her like a grown-up. In the kindest possible way, she is trying to tell her mother that she has become a woman and wants her grown-up feelings to be taken seriously.

The play addresses how painfully hard it is for Clarisse to accept Gilberte's flowering womanhood.

[*Clarisse* Gilbert . . . you know . . . this man? . . .]

Gilberte (*running to her mother, and falling on her knees beside her*) Oh, mother, yes, I had met him before! He's wanted to speak to you, ever since he came; but he didn't dare! And I didn't dare, either. It's because of me he's come to Stresa! He told me he couldn't wait so long before seeing me again. (**Clarisse** *starts.*) But there's nothing wrong, dearest mummy: there isn't, *really*! I haven't told you about it before, because I'm such a coward! And I couldn't somehow find the right moment. In Paris, we're so seldom really alone together . . . Of course, I could have, since we've been away. But you've been so worried and unhappy. I know that you're unhappy. I don't say anything about it, but I guess lots of things! . . . I expect you wonder how we met. It was at the Français. Yes, he always went to the Thursday Subscription nights. I could have introduced him to you there, but you only came once, right at the beginning. You remember how often I asked you to come with me again, but you never would. You always had something else to do at the last minute . . . Mother, we met at Lucienne's, too, five or six times! I know I ought to have told you about it before. If you knew how sorry I am that I didn't, you wouldn't be angry with me . . . I know I ought not to have gone on seeing him like that. But there seemed such lots of things that made it difficult for me to tell you. For one thing, we began to – to care for each other, just at the time that you were so troubled. Oh, dear, one never has any luck in life! . . . And, mummy, I want to tell you something . . . Oh, you're the nicest, loveliest mummy . . . but don't you still think of me as if I were a child? It hurt me dreadfully . . . it shut me up . . . Why, one day when I began to talk to you about some rather serious book, you looked at me so funnily! I just wanted to sink through the floor! . . . Well . . . I was so afraid it would be just the same if I dared to speak to you . . . about Maurice . . . (*She buries her face in her mother's lap.*)

15

Fanny's First Play
by George Bernard Shaw

This play was Shaw's biggest commercial success, running in the West End for 622 performances in 1911. It is a satirical comedy addressing issues of snobbery, middle-class morality, the gulf between the values of children and their parents, and the emptiness of 'keeping up appearances' – taking a sideswipe at theatre critics along the way!

Fanny is a well brought up, over protected Cambridge undergraduate from a wealthy family. She has written a play that is being given a private performance by professional actors as a birthday present from her father. Five eminent theatre critics have been invited along and their pretentious discussions about this 'unknown author's work' provide 'book-ends' to the performance.

Fanny's plot involves two respectable families whose well brought up children get themselves arrested and imprisoned, bringing them into contact with some 'less desirable' elements. Her theme is how the families deal with their shame and strive to maintain their social standing.

Margaret is a character in Fanny's play. She is described 'by the playwright' as the daughter of a respectable shopkeeper – 'a strong, springy girl of eighteen, with large nostrils, an audacious chin and a gaily resolute manner, even peremptory when she is annoyed.' Don't let small nostrils or a less than audacious chin put you off!

In this speech from the 'play within the play' the wayward Margaret has just spent the last two weeks in Holloway Prison. She is describing to her horrified mother the circumstance leading to her arrest: wandering the streets of London on her own; going to a theatre; picking up an attractive Frenchman; getting involved in a student brawl! I have cut her mother's shocked interpolations, but clearly Fanny intends to shock her own family in the audience with this spirited, and unrepentant story. A little later in the scene, Margaret describes herself as a 'heroine of reality' and as being 'set free from this hole of a house and all its pretences'. She revels in the feelings of liberation and power that this brings.

When the two fictional families meet at the end of Fanny's play, their expectations and assumptions are turned on their heads. It soon becomes clear that Fanny's play is a satire on her own family. Fanny herself has been arrested as a suffragette and the purpose of the play has been to try to tell them something important.

Hardly surprisingly, the same actress usually plays Fanny and Margaret.

———————

Margaret I don't know. The meeting got on my nerves, somehow. It was the singing, I suppose: you know I love singing a good swinging hymn; and I felt it was ridiculous to go home in the bus after we had been singing so wonderfully about climbing up the golden stairs to heaven. I wanted more music – more happiness – more life. I wanted some comrade who felt as I did. I felt exalted: it seemed mean to be afraid of anything: after all, what could anyone do to me against my will? I suppose I was a little mad: at all events, I got out of the bus at Piccadilly Circus, because there was a lot of light and excitement there. I walked to Leicester Square; and went into a great theatre.

[*Mrs Knox* (horrified) *A theatre!*

Margaret Yes. Lots of other women were going in alone. I had to pay five shillings.

Mrs Knox (aghast) *Five shillings!*

Margaret (apologetically) *It was a lot.*] It was very stuffy; and I didn't like the people much, because they didn't seem to be enjoying themselves; but the stage was splendid and the music lovely. I saw that Frenchman, Monsieur Duvallet, standing against a barrier, smoking a cigarette. He seemed quite happy; and he was nice and sailorlike. I went and stood beside him, hoping he would speak to me.

[*Mrs Knox* (gasps) *Margaret!*]

Margaret (*continuing*) He did, just as if he had known me for years. We got on together like old friends. He asked me would I have some champagne; and I said it would cost too much, but that I would give anything for a dance. I longed to join the people on the stage and dance with them: one of them was the most beautiful dancer I ever saw. He told me he had come there to see her, and that when it was over we could go somewhere where there was dancing. So we went to a place where there was a band in a gallery and the floor cleared for dancing. Very few people danced: the women only wanted to shew off their dresses; but we danced and danced until a lot of them joined in. We got quite reckless; and we had champagne after all. I never enjoyed anything so much. But at last it got spoilt by the

Oxford and Cambridge students up for the Boat race. They got drunk; and they began to smash things; and the police came in. Then it was quite horrible. The students fought with the police; and the police suddenly got quite brutal, and began to throw everybody downstairs. They attacked the women, who were not doing anything, and treated them just as roughly as they had treated the students. Duvallet got indignant and remonstrated with a policeman, who was shoving a woman though she was going quietly as fast as she could. The policeman flung the woman through the door and then turned on Duvallet. It was then that Duvallet swung his leg like a windmill and knocked the policeman down. And then three policemen rushed at him and carried him out by the arms and legs face downwards. Two more attacked me and gave me a shove to the door. That quite maddened me. I just got in one good bang on the mouth of one of them. All the rest was dreadful. I was rushed through the streets to the police station. They kicked me with their knees; they twisted my arms; they taunted me and insulted me; they called me vile names; and I told them what I thought of them, and provoked them to do their worst. There's one good thing about being hard hurt: it makes you sleep. I slept in that filthy cell with all the other drunks sounder than I should have slept at home. I can't describe how I felt next morning: it was hideous; but the police were quite jolly; and everybody said it was a bit of English fun, and talked about last year's boat-race night when it had been a great deal worse. I was black and blue and sick and wretched. But the strange thing was that I wasn't sorry; and I'm not sorry. And I don't feel that I did anything wrong, really. (*She rises and stretches her arms with a large liberating breath.*) Now that it's all over I'm rather proud of it; though I know now that I'm not a lady; but whether that's because we're only shopkeepers, or because nobody's really a lady except when they're treated like ladies, I don't know. (*She throws herself into a corner of the sofa.*)

Castle Wetterstein *by Frank Wedekind (translated by Stephen Spender)*

Wedekind was a vocal critic of Victorian values in nineteenth-century Europe. Ahead of his time, his expressionistic, poetic style was the forerunner of the German Expressionist Movement that followed several decades later. His subject was sex, in its many manifestations and consequently his plays were either banned for being 'pornographic' or appeared in heavily censored version. The first production of *Castle Wetterstein* was closed after a single performance in 1910.

Effie, the play's young anti-heroine, is a heartless whore – rebellious, feisty, uninhibited, untamed and driven by sensuality. At the age of fifteen she marries the Count d'Armont but when the marriage begins to stale, he encourages her to commit numerous infidelities to heighten his sexual pleasure. This sexual adventuring becomes a profession and Effie thrives on intrigue and her power over men. She is prodigiously equipped for her career!

In this scene she is talking to her distraught stepfather, Rudiger von Wetterstein. Since his marriage to Effie's mother, Rudiger has defrauded his repulsive business partner out of millions. Now, the day of reckoning has come and the partner seeks redress. He offers a deal. The price is Rudiger's wife, Leonore. Persuaded by Effie's amoral arguments, Rudiger succumbs to self-interest and agrees to the terms, in spite of Leonore's horrified objections.

Effie responds to Rudiger's despair at his predicament with this compelling piece of story telling. It is a wonderful speech full of vivid pictures, intrigue, indulgence, cunning and calculation. Look how beautifully it builds and how she engineers it all, from her clever juggling of her amorous suitors at the beginning, to her voyeuristic relish and calm exit as the Casino erupts at the end.

Paint the pictures. Indulge in the lavish imagery. Communicate the thrill of the chase and the delight in manipulation. Her message to Rudiger is this: 'Look, you have to be clever and unscrupulous to get what you want. Keep your nerve.

The end justifies the means. If you are clever you can walk coolly away from events you have engineered'.

———————————

Effie Patience, patience. Our adventures call for both intelligence and adroitness. A fortnight ago in Monte Carlo I had supper simultaneously with three different men in the same hotel without one of them having the slightest inkling of the presence of the other two. There is emotional gymnastics for you! I had to calculate in seconds. I invented excuses for my disappearances and for keeping them waiting so that my brain buzzed like a mechanical spinning-mill. Each of the three called for me at our house. Each one ordered a different dinner of five courses of which I did not let a single one go untasted. Each one brought me back to the house in his car. It was a hodge-podge of delicious mouthfuls, popping corks, journeys in motor-cars, largesse-scattering . . . The waiters had a grandstand view of the whole business. I have never been treated so respectfully and ceremoniously in any other hotel. What a strain it was next day, sorting all the events, contretemps and surprises into their proper categories. I had a slight fog of champagne on the brain, otherwise I would have drawn up a statistical table.

[*Rüdiger* (has entirely recovered his composure) *After that tour de force did you not feel your life was in danger?*

Effie What do I care about that? But just listen to the sequel.] Next day towards evening the three gentlemen go to the Casino as usual. Each one tells a large circle of friends which they carefully collect around them that at eleven o'clock the previous evening he had supper tête-à-tête with the celebrated Comtess d'Armont, or Little Monkey, as they call me, in the Hotel Méditéranée. The gentlemen furthest away from the narrators heard all three accounts. For quite a long time they keep their amusement to themselves. Suddenly the whole room bursts into a roar of laughter. Naturally my three admirers have always hated each other like poison anyhow. At first they are as if struck by lightning. All at once there comes a shout from three directions at once – 'You liars! You liars!' – Each one challenges the other two to a duel with pistols. Finally there is a tremendous scrimmage. Which was what I had been waiting for. While the bloody heads were being cooled with ice-water I permitted myself to be escorted through the rooms by the Duke of Eurasburg. No one made a single remark about me. I said to myself: how wretchedly small the great world looks when it lies at one's feet.

The Weavers *by Gerhart Hauptmann (translated by Frank Marcus)*

This play is based on historical fact. Credited as being the first 'socialist' drama, it dramatises the uprising of starving peasant weavers in the Silesian mountains in 1844. Their rebellion against exploitative manufacturers was hopelessly disorganised and easily crushed by the military. The play broke new ground in as much as the protagonists are the class of peasants, rather than an individual character.

Hauptmann came from a family of weavers so understood the deprivations of their world, although their circumstances had changed by 1893 when he wrote this. *The Weavers* is considered Hauptmann's masterpiece and brought him fame as the leading playwright of his generation.

Luise is married to Gottleib and they have a seven-year-old daughter Meilchen. Their three other children have died. She is emaciated and exhausted by a life of hunger and her toil at the loom. She lives in cramped circumstances with her aged parents in law. All the family are weavers.

News has arrived that militant weavers are running riot, have ransacked the house of Dreissiger, the exploitative local maunfacturer, and are heading their way. Meilchen has come in with a valuable silver spoon, which she found outside Dreissiger's house. Her father and grandfather demand she return it, afraid of reprisals. But to Luise the spoon represents the rare prospect of food on the table. Gottleib runs in after meeting the looters in the street. They have asked him to join them in paying back the factory owners for their brutality, but he is encouraged by his father not to get involved. Fuelled by her anger over their attitude to the spoon, Luise is beside herself at this fresh demonstration of cowardice. She doesn't pull her punches, laying first into her husband for his weakness, then ranting at her father-in-law for his inaction and useless piety. She hates the factory owners with a vengeance and blames them for her dire circumstances and the deaths of her children. She has reached the end of her tether. All the rage, grief and bitterness of a lifetime is disgorged.

The Weavers was originally written in dialect so it might

be worth considering using an accent. Maybe an accent from one of the cotton towns of the north of England would be appropriate?

───────────────

Luise (*overcome with passion and excitement, vehemently*) That's right, Gottlieb, go and crawl behind the stove. Help yourself to a spoon and put a bowl of butter-milk on your knees, change into a dress and say your prayers – then you'll be what your father wants – call yourself a man!

Laughter from the neighbours.

[**Old Hilse** (shaking with fury) *And you call yourself a woman? I'll tell you something – you may be a mother but you've got a wicked tongue. You set yourself up as an example to your child and then you push your husband into crime and lawlessness.*]

Luise (*beside herself*) You and your fine speeches . . . they won't feed my child! Thanks to that, all four of them went ragged and filthy – your words haven't dried a single nappy. Yes, I call myself a mother if you want to know and if you want to know something else I hope a plague falls on these factory-owners, I wish them to hell! Just because I am a mother – how was I to keep the poor little creatures alive? I've cried without stopping from the moment one of the poor things came into the world to when death took pity on it. You didn't care two hoots, you prayed and sang while I worked my fingers to the bone to buy a single bowl of butter-milk. All those hundreds of nights I racked my brain, wondering how I could save just one of them from the churchyard. What crime has a child committed to deserve such a miserable end – and over at Dietrich's they bathed in wine and washed in milk – no, no, when things get going here, no power on earth will hold me back. And I tell you this; if they storm Dietrich's castle – I'll be the first, and heaven help anyone who tries to stop me! – I've had enough. That's all there is to it.

[*Old Hilse* *You're a lost soul, no-one can help you.*

Luise (in a rage) *It's you that can't be helped.*] Crawlers – that's what you are, insects, but not men. You're worse than the beggars they spit at in the street, cowards that run away when they hear a baby's rattle, fools that thank their masters for giving them a beating. They've bled you so white you can't even get red in the face any more. Someone should take a whip to you and beat some life into your rotten bones. (*She goes off quickly.*)

Confusions *by Alan Ayckbourn*

Confusions is a set of five short plays with interlinking themes of confusion, isolation, conflict and misunderstanding. It was originally written as a challenge to five actors who play all parts and first performed at the Apollo Theatre in 1976.

A Talk in the Park is the final play in the set and acts as something of a curtain call.

Five lonely characters come to the park for their own personal reasons and there rehearse their preoccupations and obsessions to a neighbour on a bench. Like musical chairs, each character is driven to the next bench where they address their own obsessions before their listener moves on.

Beryl is a young, downtrodden, working class woman in an abusive relationship. She is not very bright and is living on state benefits. She has come to the park to get some peace and quiet. She is trying to concentrate on an apologetic letter she has received from her abusive partner, but has been distracted by Arthur, a lonely 'anorak', in his desperate search for company. She moves to another bench where she accosts Charles, a middle-aged businessman with his own difficulties.

Beryl's problem is that in spite of his abuse she is besotted with her partner, so always has an answer to any sensible advice to leave him. She knows from bitter experience that his excuses and promises are empty. She knows he is bound to hurt her again. The solution is obvious to everyone but Beryl. Look how she rehearses old scenarios, justifying and seeking understanding for her inability to leave. Where else can she go? How will she survive? She barely copes with life as it is. She is trapped in her miserable situation by her own inaction. Though she needs to get these feelings off her chest, all it will do is set her up for another cycle of abuse.

Beryl (*sitting*) Thanks. Sorry, only the man over there won't stop talking. I wanted to read this in peace. I couldn't concentrate. He just kept going on and on about his collections or something. I normally don't mind too much, only if you get a letter like this, you need all your concentration. You can't have people talking in your ear – especially when you're trying to decipher writing like this. He must have been stoned out of his mind when he wrote it. It wouldn't be unusual. Look at it. He wants me to come back. Some hopes. To him. He's sorry, he didn't mean to do what he did, he won't do it again I promise, etc., etc. I seem to have heard that before. It's not the first time, I can tell you. And there's no excuse for it, is there? Violence, I mean, what am I supposed to do? Keep going back to that? Every time he loses his temper he . . . I mean, there's no excuse. A fracture, you know. It was nearly a compound fracture. That's what they told me. (*Indicating her head.*) Right here. You can practically see it to this day. Two X-rays. I said to him when I got home, I said, 'You bastard, you know what you did to my head?' He just stands there. The way he does. 'Sorry,' he says, 'I'm ever so sorry.' I told him. I said, 'You're a bastard, that's what you are. A right, uncontrolled, violent, bad-tempered bastard.' You know what he said? He says, 'You call me a bastard again and I'll smash your stupid face in.' That's what he says. I mean, you can't have a rational, civilized discussion with a man like that, can you? He's a right bastard. My friend Jenny, she says, 'You're a looney, leave him for God's sake. You're a looney.' Who needs that? You tell me one person who needs that? Only where do you go? I mean, there's all my things – my personal things. All my – everything. He's even got my bloody Post Office book. I'll finish up back there, you wait and see. I must be out of my tiny mind. Eh. Sometimes I just want to jump down a deep hole and forget it. Only I know that bastard'll be waiting at the bottom. Waiting to thump the life out of me. Eh?

Sorry You've Been Troubled
by Noël Coward

Sorry You've Been Troubled is a short sketch written in 1923 for one of the famous Cochran revues. Most of it takes place on the telephone while Poppy Baker eats breakfast in bed.

Poppy is a pretty, pretentious, and predatory young social climber. She lunches with the smart 'set', wears style where her heart should be and certainly doesn't work. Almost every line tells us a little bit more about her life, her attitudes and the kind of people she mixes with. Her heartlessness, snobbery and flippancy are all transparent to an audience. Look at the telephone numbers she requests: they are all expensive London addresses or grand hotels. The one exception is her mother, who is summoned to the telephone from an upstairs room at an address in Brixton!

Poppy's main agenda is to fix up her social engagements – lunch with her circle at Ciro's and dinner with her amorous young admirer, Lieutenant Godalming – but her day is interrupted by a 'phone call from the police. It seems that her erstwhile husband has thrown himself off Westminster Bridge. It is an opportunity for attention seeking melodrama and she milks the situation for all its worth, not omitting to fill her social calendar along the way.

Although the speech has huge comic potential, it shouldn't be played for laughs. Poppy embodies everything that Coward was both obsessed with and despised about bourgeois society and manners. The comedy comes from Poppy's complete lack of self-awareness and the audience's recognition of her shallow posturing.

The whole sketch has been included so you can edit it to suit your needs and savour the punch line.

When the curtain rises **Poppy** *is discovered asleep in bed. A breakfast-tray is on a small table on her left, and a telephone on her right. Sunlight is streaming across the bed – the telephone rings violently.* **Poppy** *slowly wakes up.*

Poppy (*sleepily*) Oh damn! (*She takes off receiver and speaks with a pronounced Cockney accent.*) 'Allo! 'Allo! Who is it please? Mr Pringle— No, sir – I'm afraid Miss Baker isn't awake yet— Oh no, sir – I daren't, sir – she'd sack me on the spot, sir – yes, sir— Good-bye, sir. (*She slams down receiver crossly.*) Old fool, waking me up!

She takes the breakfast-tray from side table and rests it on her knees. She proceeds to pour out coffee, she sips some of it and then begins to eat a little toast. The telephone rings again. She takes off receiver and speaks with her mouth full.

'Allo, 'allo – who is it speaking? (*Abruptly changing her voice.*) Maggie darling, is it you?— Yes, I thought it was old Potty Pringle – twice this morning, dear, really it is the limit, he ought to be at home dandling his grandchildren— Oh yes, dear, orchids as usual – very mouldy-looking with rude speckles all over them, but still they *are* expensive – what! *No!*— You haven't got your Decree Nasty or whatever it is?— Darling, I'm frightfully glad— Well, if dragging you to the Beggar's Opera fourteen times isn't cruelty, I don't know what is— You'll have to be awfully careful now for six months, won't you?— Well, you'd better leave Claridge's and go to the Regent Palace, you'll be safer there— Do you mean to say the Judge actually said that to you in Court?— What a dreadful old man – but they're all the same, dear, no respect for one's finer feelings— Fanny? Oh no, it was quite different with her, she won her case on points like a boxer— No, nothing was ever proved because though she started for Brighton four times with the worst possible intentions, she never got further than Haywards Heath— Well, dear, I really am most awfully glad— I suppose they'll give you the custody of the Daimler— What? Oh no, darling, no such luck, I heard from him yesterday – he won't let me divorce him— Beast!— It isn't as if we were fond of one another, I haven't set eyes on him for five years— Yes, he's with Freda Halifax now, she got him away from Vera – I

believe she'd driving him mad – serve him right – what I think of
husbands!— Oh no, Bobbie's different – besides, he isn't yet, I don't
suppose he ever will be. (*She sniffs.*) You know, I love him terribly—
Don't go on giggling— All right, Ciro's at one o'clock.

*She puts receiver on and resumes her breakfast. Her expression is rather
pensive and she occasionally sniffs pathetically. The telephone rings
again, she answers it.*

Hallo— Hallo— Yes, who is it?— What?— I can't hear. What? Oh,
the line's buzzing— Yes, yes, speaking— Police station! Why – what's
happened?— Yes— Last night— Oh, my God! – this is terrible— Yes,
at twelve o'clock— I say – listen— Oh, they've cut me off!

*She puts the receiver on again and sits in stricken silence for a moment.
She bites her lip and dabs her eyes with her handkerchief; then a thought
strikes her – she grabs the telephone.*

Hallo— Exchange – get me Mayfair 7160 at once— Yes—
Claridge's?— Put me through to Mrs. Fanshawe, please— Oh, quick,
quick, it's urgent— Hallo— Maggie— Maggie, is that you?— Oh, my
dear, listen, the most awful thing – the police have just rung up—
Jim jumped over Waterloo Bridge last night— No, darling, I don't
know what time— Yes, I knew you'd be sympathetic— That's a little
callous of you, dear; remember he *was* my husband after all— I'm
wretched – utterly wretched— Yes, naturally they communicated
with me first, how were they to know we hadn't seen each other for
years?— Oh, it's awful – awful! Yes, Ciro's one o'clock. (*She hangs up
receiver for a moment, then bangs lever violently.*) Hallo— Hallo—
Kensington 8712 – yes, quickly. Hallo, is that you, Flossie? Poppy
speaking— My dear, Jim's dead! (*She sniffs.*) Thank you, darling, I
knew you'd be a comfort— No, dear, he jumped off Waterloo
Bridge— Yes, the one next to Charing Cross— No, no, no, *that's*
Blackfriars. Don't be so silly, Flossie, you know perfectly well
Westminster comes first, then Charing Cross – the one with trains
on it, *then* Waterloo— Oh, how *can* you – you do say the most
dreadful things, you'll only make me break down again in a minute
– I'm having such a struggle – such a bitter, bitter struggle— (*She*

sobs.) Anyhow, I'm quite successful enough without that kind of advertisement— Look here, lunch with Maggie and me at Ciro's one o'clock— All right – *thank you*, darling. (*She hangs up receiver again. Then after a moment's pause she calls up.*) Hallo, hallo, Regent 2047, please – yes – I want to speak to Miss Hancox, please— Yes, it's important— Hallo, is that you, Violet? Poppy speaking. You know when you told my cards the other day you told me something dreadful was going to happen? Well, it has!— Oh, no, darling, not *that*; anyhow I haven't seen him since Tuesday – no, no, much worse— Jim's dead. Yes, dead— I know, dear, I try to look at it in that light, but it's very very hard – you see, after all, he was my husband— I know three months wasn't long, but still– You do say divine things – it wasn't very kind of him, was it?— Well, dear, Maggie and Flossie and I are lunching at Ciro's at one – come too, and we'll talk it all over then. Good-bye.

She hangs up receiver and then rings up again.

Hallo, Hallo, Exchange— Mayfair 6773, please – yes— Hallo, is that the Guards Club – yes, put me through to Lieutenant Godalming, please – yes please— (*She puts the receiver down for a moment while she takes puff from under her pillow and powders her nose – then she speaks again.*) Hallo, is that you, darling?— Oh, I'm sorry, Higgins, I thought it was Lieutenant Godalming – in his bath?— Please, please get him out of it, Higgins, it's frightfully important— Yes, I'll hold on— (*There is a pause.*) Darling – something too fearful has happened – yes, absolutely appalling – Jim's dead. What – who's Jim? He's my husband, of course – yes, he jumped off Waterloo Bridge last night— *He jumped off Waterloo Bridge last night. No! Waterloo Bridge!* Your ears must be full of soap— Isn't it dreadful?— Now, Bobbie dear, you mustn't be naughty— No, darling, I won't listen to you – I'm very, very miserable – it's been a terrible shock— Very well, I'll forgive you— Kiss me, then. (*She responds to his kisses over the telephone.*) Yes, tonight – somewhere quiet – really quiet – really quiet – I shan't have any appetite— No, that would be too heartless— No, that would be too dull— Say the Embassy— All right, good-bye, darling – Bobbly wobbly—

She hangs up receiver and rings up again.

Hallo— Brixton 8146, please— Hallo, is that you, Mr Isaacstein? It's Miss Baker speaking – will you fetch my mother down, please— Yes, it's important. (*A slight pause.*) Is that you, Mum?— What do you think, Jim's been and drowned himself— I don't know – I expect Freda drove him to it— No, Mother, I won't have you saying things like that – besides, he's too young to marry yet— Look here, Flossie, Violet, Maggie and I are lunching at Ciro's— One o'clock – come along too and we'll talk it over— You can wear that old one of mine— All right.

She rings off and screams for her **Maid**.

Lily – Lilee – come here—

She pushes breakfast-tray to end of the bed and is just about to spring out when her **Maid** *enters, sobbing bitterly.*

What is it?— What's the matter with you?

Lily It's dreadful, dreadful—

Poppy What's dreadful?

Lily That poor dear upstairs—

Poppy Mrs Straker?

Lily Yes, Mrs Straker – she's just heard that her husband jumped off Waterloo Bridge last night.

Poppy What!!

The telephone rings violently. **Poppy** *snatches up the receiver, listens for a moment, then hurls the instrument to the floor.*

(*Through clenched teeth.*) Sorry you've been troubled!

The Good Woman of Setzuan
by Bertolt Brecht (translated by Eric Bentley)

The Good Woman of Setzuan is a parable about capitalism set in the poor half-westernised Chinese city of Setzuan. Brecht was a Marxist who saw theatre as an instrument for political and social change. The play was written during his exile in America during the Second World War.

In the play three gods come to earth with a mission. Their 'jobs' depend on finding one truly good human being, but they find a world riddled with swindlers, rascals and self-interest. Only a young prostitute, Shen Te, seems to fit the bill. To encourage her virtue, they give her money that she uses to buy a small tobacco shop. The poor citizens of Setzuan make such demands on her generous nature, however, that she is forced to invent a ruthless alter ego, cousin Shui Ta, to survive. As business expands, Shui Ta takes over from Shen Te and the citizens of Setzuan become suspicious of Shen Te's lengthy absences. Believing Shui Ta has murdered her, the case is brought to court where the gods, disguised as judges, preside. Confronted by the conflicting evidence of the citizens, Shen Te is forced to admit her dual identity. She tears off Shui Ta's disguise and makes this impassioned confession.

Shen Te is an innocent, who longs to do good, but has to split herself in two in order to deal with the complex demands life makes on her. The speech is written in short plain lines. Observe the line endings and you will find its simple measure.

Brecht had interesting theories about the theatre and the way in which actors should approach his characters. He saw the actors' job as being not only to inhabit their characters but also to retain a degree of detachment from them. In this way the audience not only identifies with the character's emotional journey, but is also aware of watching a theatrical performance with a message. This should be borne in mind when you are studying the text, although your chief concern should be to play Shen Te's moral dilemmas and her anguish at failing the god's expectations.

Shen Te is the mouthpiece through which Brecht asks us to consider what the individual can do to make the world a better place.

Shui Ta I have a terrible confession to make: I am she! (*He takes off his mask, and tears away his clothes.* **Shen Te** *stands there.*

Shen Te Shen Te, yes. Shui Ta *and* Shen Te. Both.
Your injunction
To be good and yet to live
Was a thunderbolt:
It has torn me in two
I can't tell how it was
But to be good to others
And myself at the same time
I could not do it
Your world is not an easy one, illustrious ones!
When we extend our hand to a beggar, he tears it off for us
When we help the lost, we are lost ourselves
And so
Since not to eat is to die
Who can long refuse to be bad?
As I lay prostrate beneath the weight of good intentions
Ruin stared me in the face
It was when I was unjust that I ate good meat
And hob-nobbed with the mighty
Why?
Why are bad deeds rewarded?
Good ones punished?
I enjoyed giving
I truly wished to be the Angel of the Slums
But washed by a foster-mother in the water of the gutter
I developed a sharp eye
The time came when pity was a thorn in my side
And, later, when kind words turned to ashes in my mouth

And anger took over
I became a wolf
Find me guilty, then, illustrious ones,
But know:
All that I have done I did
To help my neighbour
To help my lover
And to keep my little one from want
For your great, godly deeds, I was too poor, too small.

Camille *by Pam Gems*

Pam Gems' feminist version of Alexandre Dumas the younger's much adapted novel, *La Dame aux Camelias,* is set in Paris in the mid 1880s. It is the mythic story of a whore, Marguerite Gautier, who falls in love with an aristocrat, Armand Duval but leaves him rather than allow the scandal of their liaison to ruin his life. Beset by creditors, she dies a lonely death from consumption – the tragic price for her self-sacrifice.

Marguerite is a strong, feisty, erotic beauty who, after a childhood of poverty and sexual abuse, has become a high class, much sought-after courtesan.

In this scene, she and Armand are in her bedroom after making love. They are sharing intimacies – trading honesty for honesty as lovers do. Armand insists on knowing every last thing about her. He quizzes her about her illegitimate child and how she came to live the life of a courtesan. Her response is fiery as she is stung into memories of an abusive childhood and into drawing stark parallels between her impoverished beginnings and his privilege. If that is what he wants then she will tell him everything. She seems to be both accusing him and challenging him to understand.

She describes how she yearned for the beautiful things she saw in the house where she worked as a housemaid, and how her master exercised his *droit du seigneur* when she was thirteen, making her pregnant. She relates how she was dismissed in consequence of her pregnancy and tells of the eye-opening moment when she discovered what an asset her body could be. Painful realities – like separation from her son – are touched on lightly, or laughed at defensively as if to do otherwise would open deep wounds. Objectivity and matter-of-factness allow distance from the pain of shocking events.

Marguerite has learned to survive in a tough world, which has given her a tigerish independence. She tells her story with candour, insight and without a scrap of self-pity. This is a woman whose background, class and experience have left her no option but to take control of her own life in the only way she knows.

Pam Gems' stage directions are very useful here, giving excellent insights into Marguerite's shifts of mood.

Marguerite You want to know? You want to know? What do you know? I know the way you live! Hot-house grapes, lofts full of apples, figs with the bloom on them . . . stables, libraries, a fire in your room. (*She lopes, fiery and restless.*) I used to clean the grates with my mother . . . five o'clock in the morning on tiptoe while you all snored. I saw them! The rugs, the pictures, the furniture . . . chandeliers . . . music rooms, ballrooms . . . all a hundred metres from where we lived on potatoes and turnips, and slept, the seven of us together in a coach-house loft.

[*Armand* (slight pause) *Are you accusing me?*

Marguerite Yes.*]

Pause.

Marguerite At thirteen, I became a housemaid. I slept in an attic . . . in my own bed, you can't believe the bliss! I couldn't wait to get up in the morning! To be in such a palace . . .

Pause.

He shakes her gently to make her continue. She looks at him and away.

After two years *Monsieur le Marquis* took me into his bed. It was his habit with the younger maids. It kept him young. A year later I had our son.

She plays with the quilt for a moment then speaks with musing objectivity.

You have no idea what difference a child makes. Your life is quite changed. For ever. Of course, with a man, this can never happen. Not in the same way.

[*Armand* How do you mean?*]

Marguerite You're no longer alone. You're connected . . . with someone who is, and isn't you. Your own flesh. I love my brothers of course . . . but . . . you grow up . . . you go away, you're on your own. Until, if you're a woman, you have a child. Then you're never alone again. Whether you wish it or not . . . whether you see the child or not. It's there. Part of you. Of your body. You have reason . . . purpose – oh, no destiny too fine, for the child!

Pause.

(*Light*) I hardly ever see him. He thinks I'm his aunt.

She pauses . . . then, as **Armand** *starts to speak.*

I was dismissed, of course. I went to my mother's sister and sat by the river wondering what to do. I had no money. The most sensible thing seemed to be to drown myself.

Pause.

And then, one morning . . . my cousin came into my room. I was putting on my stockings – he started to shake. I didn't have the strength to push him away. Afterwards, he put his finger to his lips, and gave me a gold coin.

And there it was. I knew. All of a sudden. How to do it. How to go through the magic door. How to be warm, how to be comfortable . . . eat fine food, wear fine clothes, read fine books, listen to fine music. I had the key. A golden key. (*She laughs.*)

The Bald Prima Donna *by Eugene Ionesco (translated by Donald Watson)*

Rumanian-born Eugene Ionesco is considered to be the father of absurdist theatre. His work was banned in his native country so he spent much of his adult life in France where, in the 1950s, he became one of the leading dramatists of the French avant-garde. *The Bald Prima Donna* is his first play and was inspired by the empty clichés he found in a phrase book while teaching himself English. The play explores the absurdities of human interaction through the deadly exchanges of a suburban couple. It is a surreal satire on the shallowness of bourgeois life.

Two dinner guests visit 'typically English' Mr and Mrs Smith in their 'typically English' home in a 'typically English' suburb, where they then exchange platitudes about the most banal, meaningless matters. The visiting couple feels they have met one another somewhere before. When they discover they not only live in the same house and sleep in the same bed under the same green eiderdown and both have a little daughter called Alice, they reach the conclusion that they must be husband and wife. As they kiss and fall asleep in the same armchair, Mary, the Smith's maid, tiptoes in to throw things into disarray.

Mary is a young 'below stairs', 'dear little thing' stereotype. She addresses the audience directly, speaking in hushed, confidential tones so as not to wake the sleeping pair. Absurdity is piled upon absurdity and conventional reality flies out of the window as Mary plays detective to get to the bottom of the couple's identities. You can almost hear the unspoken 'elementary, my dear Watson' as she sets out her evidence.

There is no heavy subtext to the play or background story to explore. Your challenge is how to flesh out the stereotype. Mary is a caricature of a maid playing a caricature of a detective. The humour comes from the total absurdity of the situation and Mary's use of the most convoluted tongue-twisting language to deliver her proofs. You must draw your audience into a world that has its own insane symmetry and logic.

Mary Elizabeth and Donald are now far too happy to be able to hear me. So I can tell you a secret. Elizabeth is not Elizabeth and Donald is not Donald. And I'll prove it to you. The child Donald talked of is not Elizabeth's daughter, not the same child at all. Donald's little girl has one red eye and one white eye just like Elizabeth's little girl. But whereas it's the right eye of Donald's child that's red and the left eye that's white, it's the left eye of Elizabeth's child that's red and the right eye that's white. Consequently the whole fabric of Donald's argumentation falls to the ground, when it encounters this final obstacle, which annihilates his entire theory. In spite of the extraordinary coincidence, which would appear incontrovertible evidence to the contrary, as Donald and Elizabeth are not after all the parents of the same child, they are not, in fact, Donald and Elizabeth. Donald may well believe he is Donald; Elizabeth may well think she is Elizabeth. Donald may well believe her to be Elizabeth; Elizabeth may well think him to be Donald: they are both grievously deceived. But who is the real Donald? Which is the real Elizabeth? Who can possibly be interested in prolonging this misunderstanding? I haven't the slightest idea. Let us make no attempt to find out. Let us leave things strictly alone.

She takes several steps towards the door, then returns and addresses the audience again.

My real name is Sherlock Holmes.

Wine in the Wilderness *by Alice Childress*

The work of black dramatist Alice Childress is characterised by her frank and controversial treatment of race issues. This play was first produced in an American TV series in 1969. It explores the demand on black people to present positive images of themselves in their lives and art. The original broadcast was banned throughout the entire state of Alabama.

The play is set in the Harlem studio of Bill Jameson, a middle-class black artist, at the time of the 1964 race riots. Bill is painting a triptych called *Wine in the Wilderness* as his personal statement on 'black womanhood'. He has already painted innocent 'black girlhood' and iconic 'black womanhood in her noblest form'. Now he needs a model for a modern antithesis – a grass roots woman 'that's had her behind kicked until its numb'. To this end, his middle-class friends, writer Sonny-Man and social worker Cynthia, bring round Tommy, a homeless factory worker whose flat has just been torched in the riots.

Tommy (short for Tomorrow Marie) is born and bred in Harlem. She is just thirty, big-hearted, brash, edgy, vulnerable, streetwise and uneducated. She is dressed in a mismatched skirt and sweater and wears a cheap wig. All her other possessions have been destroyed in the fire. Her big dream is to find a man 'who will treat her halfway decent'. Bill looks a promising candidate and she agrees to pose for him, not realising how he wants to represent her. She is flattered at being accepted into his world, but when she discovers Bill wants to paint her as 'a messed up chick', not glorious 'Mother Africa', she is outraged and humiliated. She lashes out at Bill's patronising attitudes and for treating her like a 'nigger'.

Here her anger is all but spent and she preparing to leave, to go back to the place she belongs. It is an eloquent, deeply-felt speech driven by Tommy's new-found sense of identity. She's talking back and walking tall. Her attack on Bill's condescending attitudes shames him into a new awareness. He sees that his picture of the beautiful African queen, 'Wine in the Wilderness'; is based on an empty figment of his imagination, and he realises too the distance he has travelled from the beauty of his fellow real-life black Americans.

Childress' affirmative ending sees Bill preparing to paint a new triptych with Tommy as its centrepiece.

Tommy I don't stay mad, it's here today and gone tomorrow. I'm sorry your feelin's got hurt, . . . but when I'm hurt I turn and hurt back. Somewhere, in the middle of last night, I thought the old me was gone, . . . lost forever, and gladly. But today was flippin' time, so back I flipped. Now it's 'turn the other cheek' time. If I can go through life other-cheekin' the white folk, . . . guess yall can be other-cheeked too. But I'm goin' back to the nitty-gritty crowd, where the talk is we-ness and us-ness. I hate to do it but I have to thank you 'cause I'm walkin' out with much more than I brought in. (*Goes over and looks at the queen in the 'Wine In The Wilderness' painting.*) Tomorrow-Marie had such a lovely yesterday. (**Bill** *takes her hand, she gently removes it from his grasp.*) Bill, I don't have to wait for anybody's by-your-leave to be a 'Wine In The Wilderness' woman. I can be it if I wanta, . . . and I *am*. I am. I am. I'm not the one you made up and painted, the very pretty lady who can't talk back, . . . but I'm 'Wine In The Wilderness' . . . alive and kickin', me . . . Tomorrow-Marie, cussin' and fightin' and lookin' out for my damn self 'cause ain' nobody else 'round to do it, dontcha know. And, Cynthia, if my hair is straight, or if it's natural, or if I wear a wig, or take it off, . . . that's all right; because wigs . . . shoes . . . hats . . . bags . . . and even this . . . (*She picks up the African throw she wore a few moments before . . . fingers it.*) They're just what you call . . . access . . . (*Fishing for the word.*) . . . like what you wear with your Easter outfit . . .

[*Cynthia Accessories.*

Tommy Thank you, my sister.] Accessories. Somethin' you add on or take off. The real thing is takin' place on the inside . . . that's where the action is. That's 'Wine In The Wilderness', . . . a woman that's a real one and a good one. And yall just better believe I'm it. (*She proceeds to the door.*)

Eden Cinema *by Marguerite Duras*
(translated by Barbara Bray)

This play was adapted by Marguerite Duras from her third novel *Un Barrage contre le Pacifique*, published in France in 1950. It was first produced by the Renaud-Barrault Company in Paris in 1977. It is a play about memory and the destructive power of love, and is largely based on Duras' own experiences of growing up in colonial French Indo-China. It is a stylised, retrospective piece in which the characters reveal their inner lives directly to the audience while also participating in the action.

The Mother, a French widow, has been cheated out of her savings which she invested in a worthless tract of flooded salt plain on the west coast of Cambodia. Her struggle against poverty and her efforts to protect her rice paddies by erecting walls to hold back the Pacific, provides a powerful metaphor for her futile attempts to hold her family together. Her children, Suzanne and Joseph, trapped by the Mother and their circumstances, are the narrators of her story.

It begins with the Mother's purchase of the bad land in 1924 and follows the family fortunes until the mother's death. As the story unravels, family tensions are laid bare.

Desperate to alleviate the family's poverty, the Mother pushes Suzanne into the arms of Mr Jo, heir to rich rubber plantations in Northern Cambodia. Mr Jo is besotted with Suzanne but won't marry her because of family objections. The Mother says 'marriage or nothing', so a desperate Mr Jo tries to blackmail her, giving her a valuable diamond rather than face losing Suzanne altogether.

At this point Suzanne, 'made up like a tart', has gone with her mother and brother to the city to sell the diamond to finance a new sea wall. But the diamond turns out to be flawed and worth only half the asking price. We feel Suzanne's frustration and sense her anxiety for her mother's sanity as she watches her growing obsession and irrational rejection of all reasonable offers for the stone. She knows her mother's battle with the ocean is unhinging her mind. Suzanne relates with despair and disbelief her mother's fruitless and vengeful hunt for Mr Jo, her failure to sell the diamond and her attempts to sell her into prostitution instead.

The sting in the tail of the speech should be stark and terrible as Suzanne realises that what matters most to her mother is money to build a new sea wall. Look how Suzanne distances herself from events by referring in the abstract to 'the' mother at the beginning of the speech, then reverting to the personal pronoun by the end when the pain becomes deeply personal. She must free herself of her love for her mother if she is to escape her destructive power.

Suzanne The Central Hotel looked out on the Mekong River on one side, and on the other, on the tramway between Cholen and Saigon. The hotel was run by Carmen, Mademoiselle Marthe's daughter. Mademoiselle Marthe had worked in a brothel in Saigon harbour. She'd bought the hotel for her daughter.

Both Mademoiselle Marthe and Carmen were very fond of the mother. For years they'd let her stay in the hotel for nothing. Now, again, Carmen had tried to help her. She'd tried to sell the diamond to the guests staying in the hotel. But none of them would buy it. So, the mother decided to sell the diamond herself.

The first dealer she takes it to offers her ten thousand piastres.

He says it's got a serious flaw, what's known in the trade as a 'toad'. It halves its value. The mother doesn't believe it. She wants twenty thousand piastres. She goes to another dealer. Then to a third, then to a fourth. They all point out the toad. The mother persists. She still wants twenty thousand piastres. The less they offer the more she wants her twenty thousand. Twenty thousand piastres is what the new sea-wall will cost, the one she wants to build before she dies. She's offered eleven thousand piastres. Six thousand. Eight thousand. She refuses. This goes on for a week. She goes out every morning when it gets dark. First she goes to the white dealers. Then to the others. The Indians. And finally to the Chinese in Cholen.

For a week Joseph and I wait for her to come out of the dealers' shops. Then, one evening, Joseph doesn't come back to the hotel. He's gone off in the Citroën. The mother doesn't pay much attention to Joseph's disappearance. She's obsessed with the diamond. She's already beginning to identify Mr Jo with the 'toad' in the heart of the diamond.

Silence.

[**Suzanne** smiles at the **Mother**. The **Mother** looks at her. This interruption of their stillness must be performed in silence. It's as if the **Mother** were trying to remember something.

Mother *'I ought to have been suspicious of that toad right from the beginning. Right from the moment I met him in the bar at Réam.'*

The **Mother** smiles.]

Suzanne's Voice And then, one evening, she gets it into her head that she must find Mr. Jo.

Music.

She tells me *she'll* find Mr. Jo in the city, and then she'll bring him to me. I promise the mother to ask him for the two other diamonds he showed me out on the plain. The mother waits for Mr. Jo outside cinemas. Looks for him in cafés, outside luxury shops, in hotel lobbies. She never finds him.

Pause.

Suzanne *gets up and moves away from the* **Mother**.

The **Mother** *remains alone.*

Suzanne *looks at her. The* **Mother** *doesn't move.*

It should be a terrible moment.

Suzanne So what did she do, my mother? She tried to sell me instead of the diamond. She asked Carmen to find a man who would take me far away, for every. The mother want to be alone.

50

The **Mother** *slowly turns and looks at* **Suzanne**. *A shattering look denying nothing, excusing nothing.*

Pause.

She doesn't want children any more.

Saint's Day *by John Whiting*

John Whiting's apocalyptic drama *Saint's Day*, written in the late 1940s, is rich with poetic symbolism. It was praised and lambasted by the critics in equal measure, but is now seen as a flawed masterpiece that cleared the ground for writers like Beckett, Pinter and Bond.

The play addresses two themes: the isolation of the artist and the violence that lives beneath the surface of a civilised society.

Stella Heberden is a plain, lonely, insecure thirty-two-year-old with a husband who is twelve years her junior. She is pregnant. She lives with two men: Paul Southman, her grandfather and her husband Charles, who is a painter. Paul was once a famous poet and writer, but twenty-five years earlier was driven into literary exile after publishing a satirical pamphlet on the abolition of printing; while as a matter of principle Charles refuses to sell his paintings. Both men are artists who have effectively exiled themselves from society, trapping Stella with them in a chilly old house on the outskirts of a village that has been made hostile by her grandfather's behaviour.

Stella is keen to restore her grandfather's literary reputation so as to secure a future for her unborn child and bring in some much needed income. Her plans are beginning to bear fruit as they await a visit from the Honourable Robert Procathren, a distinguished young poet and critic who is coming to whisk Paul off to a big public celebration of his eighty-third birthday.

John Winter, the family's elderly man-servant, has been dispatched to the village to buy food for the visitor. At this point he has just returned with the ominous news that militant soldiers have escaped from the local detention camp and are terrorising the village. Paul sees the soldiers as his natural allies, discussing with John Winter how the household can form an alliance with the soldiers against the villagers.

The pair's childish schemes and ridiculous military language horrify Stella. She has lived with the villagers' animosity since childhood and understands the very real dangers of their situation, one which her grandfather's attitudes can only exacerbate. Dispatching Paul to bed in preparation for his trip, she spells out the danger to Charles who has sided with her grandfather. The speech is both explanation and appeal. She describes the fragile peace that exists between the family and the villagers, blaming her splenetic grandfather for provoking a dangerous situation. With eerie prescience she recognises that matters are coming to a head. Frightened and desperate to be free of the house and the spectre of violence, she appeals to Charles for his support. She is clutching at straws but sees this visitor from the outside world as the agent of their salvation.

With supreme irony, the play spirals into tragedy when Stella is killed by her 'saviour' Procathren in a gun accident and the soldiers break into the house. Their visitor's civilised veneer crumbles as he joins the prevailing forces of violence and chaos, hanging Robert and Charles from the trees outside the house.

Stella [*No, you're to rest.* (**Paul** and **John Winter** have gone up the stairs.)] Did you hear them? Ridiculous! Two old men with their stupid attempts at military phrases and reports. Did you hear them? 'Situation – immediate danger – diversion – an alliance.'

[*Charles Yes, I heard them.*

Stella Absurd!

Charles But I thought – I may have been mistaken – I thought that you appreciated a very real danger from the villagers.

Stella I do. It is a very real danger.] If the villagers could organize themselves, or could be moved by a moment's rage they would come here and kill us all. At present they suffer from no more than a grievance. And they have cause – they have cause for grievance and for hating us. When Paul came here- when he withdrew himself from the world that attacked him – he chose the village to be his butt. I remember the things he said – (*She has taken two loose cigarettes from the pocket of her dress. She throws one to* **Charles.**) – here

54

– catch! – I remember the things he said about the village when I was a child – unforgivable, beastly and unprovoked. Paul was then no longer in a position to attack his equals and so his abuse, the result of hurt pride, was directed against the villagers. It was unprovoked because he had no quarrel with them but for their sanity and security. Soon they felt – under his attack – they felt their security gone and with it their sanity. The satire that had recently shaken the world was directed against them – against a few miserable peasants in a ramshackle hamlet. They reacted in the way of the world, and as Paul would say, 'declared war on us'. That war has continued since my childhood. It has coloured my life – the threat of violence to this tortured family. And so, Charles, I am frightened to hear such nonsense talked by Paul – with encouragement from John Winter – when we need expert and serious conspiracy to save our lives. Reason tells us that we cannot fight the villagers – we cannot do it, and so we must get away – run away if you like. This is what we must do. But how? I can do nothing – you can do nothing – we are useless, helpless and wretched and must appeal to the one man capable of saving us – Procathren. I know! I know he is a poor specimen in your eyes, but we must appeal to him. He may help us. You must admit that we need help, and I have no pride in such matters. I have no pride at all. But try to remember, Charles, that I am a woman – try to be conscious of that at other times than when I am naked. I am a woman and I have a child inside me. Does that explain anything to you? Pregnant women have delusions, they say. Do they? I know nothing about it. Am I deluded, Charles? Am I?

The Unexpected Guest *by Agatha Christie*

This is a murder mystery written by the queen of crime writers, Agatha Christie. It was first performed at the Duchess Theatre in 1958. Ingenious plot twists, colourful characters and surprise endings were her stock in trade and this play is no exception. Although the style is very much of its period, Christie still has considerable appeal – witness *The Mousetrap* which has run in London's West End since 1952!

The action is set in Richard Warwick's book-lined study in his house in South Wales. When the curtain rises, Laura Warwick, a stylish, upper-class, attractive blonde of about thirty, is discovered with a gun in her hand. Beside her is the dead body of her wheelchair-bound husband. She is confronted by Michael Starkwedder who has come in through the French windows to look for help, having driven his car into a ditch in the fog – or so we are led to believe. Laura appears to have been caught red-handed, and she confesses to the murder. Rather than calling the police, Starkwedder pours her a drink and then goes through the evening's events with her, quizzing her like a barrister and gently leading her towards the idea that there might be some way out of her predicament. It soon emerges that Warwick was a loathsome drunkard who was frightening to live with and hated by everyone.

Calmed by a drink, a cigarette and Starkwedder's cool charm, the shell-shocked Laura is drawn into telling him more about her marriage and her husband's nature. As the narrative unfolds, Laura relaxes into it, caught up in her recollections of her husband's destructive nature and her bitterness towards him. It should be remembered that all the time her husband's body is close by and she is talking to a complete stranger who seems to hold her destiny in his hands.

But who is the real murderer? Who is Laura protecting? True to form, the final twist in Christie's plot is as unexpected as the appearance and identity of the guest from the play's title.

Laura We married soon after we met. Then two years later he had a terrible accident – he was mauled by a lion. He was lucky to escape alive, but he's been a semi-cripple ever since, unable to walk properly. (*She leans back, more relaxed.*)

Starkwedder *sits on the stool, facing her.*

They say misfortune improves your character. It didn't improve his. Instead, it developed all his bad points. Vindictiveness, a streak of sadism, drinking too much. He made life pretty impossible for everyone in this house, and we all put up with it because – oh, you know what one says. 'So sad for poor Richard being an invalid.' We shouldn't have, of course. I see that now. It encouraged him to feel that he was different from other people, that he could do as he chose without being called to account for it. (*She rises and crosses to the table by the armchair down* L, *to flick ash in the ashtray.*) All his life, shooting had been the thing he liked doing best. So every night after we went up to bed he'd sit here, and Angell, his valet-attendant, would bring the brandy and one of his guns and put them beside him. Then he'd have this window wide open and he'd sit here looking out watching for the gleam of a cat's eyes or a stray rabbit, or a dog. Of course, there haven't been so many rabbits lately. But he shot quite a lot of cats. He shot them in the daytime, too. And birds.

[*Starkwedder Didn't the neighbours ever complain?*

Laura (crossing to the sofa and sitting C again) *Oh, naturally.*] We've only lived here for a couple of years, you know. Before that we lived on the east coast, in Norfolk. One or two household pets were victims there and there were a lot of complaints. That's really why we came to live here. It's very isolated, this house. We've only one neighbour in miles. But there are plenty of cats and squirrels and birds. (*A pause, then she goes on.*) The trouble in Norfolk was really because a woman came to call one day for subscriptions for the vicarage fête. Richard sent shots to right and left of her as she was going away down the drive. She bolted like a hare, he said. He roared with laughter when he told us about it. Her fat backside was quivering like a jelly, he said. However, she went to the police about it and there was a terrible row.

[*Starkwedder I can well imagine that.*]

Laura But Richard got away with it all right. He had a permit for all his firearms and he explained he only used them to shoot rabbits. He explained away Miss Butterfield as a nervous old maid convinced that he was shooting at *her*, which, of course, was all nonsense. Richard was always plausible. He made them believe him.

The Devils *by John Whiting*

The themes of this play are sexual repression, mass hysteria, religious bigotry and political intrigue during the witch-hunts of seventeenth-century France.

The action takes place mainly in the town of Loudun, and briefly in Paris, between 1623 and 1634. It is based on Aldous Huxley's book, *The Devils of Loudon*, which will be useful for your research. It was first performed by the Royal Shakespeare Company in 1961 and subsequently adapted as a controversial film, directed by Ken Russell, that you will also find useful.

The central character Urbain Grandier is a charismatic young priest whose libertarian views bring him into conflict with the Church hierarchy and lead to accusations of witchcraft. For these he is ultimately tried, tortured and burned at the stake.

Sister Jeanne is the unusually young Prioress of St Ursula's convent. She is a commanding, bitter, little woman with a hunched back, whose relationship with her God is rooted in duty rather than piety. She has formed an erotic fixation on Grandier who has thwarted her by refusing her invitation to become Director of the convent. On receiving his letter, she is bitterly disappointed. Tearing it in half, she presses it to her body as if it were Grandier himself.

Left alone, her sexual passion for Grandier manifests itself in this masturbation fantasy in which she jealously envisages Grandier having sex with the local magistrate's daughter. Her imagination conjures the scene in vivid, painful detail, but the lyrical language is counter-pointed with self-loathing and scorn as she wrestles with her confusion about the powerful new feelings she is experiencing. She is the voyeur of a fantasy that both disgusts and titillates in spite of her resistance. The question about the 'divine mystery' of love she poses at the beginning of the speech is answered in a convulsion of pleasure as she orgasms at the end – bringing her face to face with her unfulfilled desires and the sterility of her life.

It will be Sister Jeanne's evidence that Grandier has possessed her with demons that finally seals his fate,

destroying that which she loves most out of guilt and
perversity.

Jeanne What is this divine mystery? Let me see. Let me see.
(*Laughter.*) I was about to address myself to God in this matter.
Habit. Habit. It would never do. No. It must be to Man.

She whispers the name: 'Grandier.'

You wake up. Dawn has broken over others before you. Look at the
little grey window. Then turn. She lies beside you. The attitude is of
prayer or the womb. Her mouth tastes of wine and the sea. Her skin
is smooth and silky, rank with sweat. The native odours of her body
have exhausted in the night the scents of day.

Phillipe, *naked, is seen making love with* **Grandier**. *They will continue
to be seen in the touching formal attitudes of passion throughout*
Jeanne*'s words.*

Jeanne Look down at her. What do you feel? Sadness? It must be
sadness. You are a man. Ah, now she stretches her arms above her
head. Are you not moved? This is not the sophistry of a whore,
whatever you may pretend. She shifts her legs, entwines them, lays
a finger on your lips and her mouth upon her finger. She whispers.
Those words were taught. She only repeats the lesson. Such filth is
love to her, and the speaking of it is an act of faith. (*Sudden
laughter.*) What was that you did? Stretching out to clutch the falling
bedclothes. Was it to cover your nakedness? Is there modesty here?

(*Silence: in wonder.*) How strange. Can you laugh, too? That's
something I didn't know. Pain, oblivion, unreason, mania. These I
thought would be in your bed. But laughter . . .

How young you both look. Quiet again.

The girl is heavy in your arms. She yawned, and you have taken up
the shudder of her body. You tremble, in spite of yourself. Look, the
sun is breaking up the mists in the fields. You're going to be

engulfed by day. Take what you can. Let both take what they can. Now.

Now.

(*She weeps.*) This frenzy, this ripping apart, this meat on a butcher's slab. Where are you? Love? Love? What are you? Now. Now. Now.

Jeanne *falls on her knees, convulsed.* **Grandier** *and* **Philippe** *can no longer be seen.*

Jeanne (*suffocated, young voice*) O my God, is that it? Is that it?

Darkness.

K D Dufford hears K D Dufford ask K D Dufford how K D Dufford'll make K D Dufford *by David Halliwell*

K. D. Dufford (to cut a long title short) is a dark surreal mixture of comedy and cruelty. It's a complex 'multi-viewpoint' play in which versions of the same event are replayed from different perspectives. It was written around the time of the Moors Murders in the 1960s, and tells the almost intolerable tale of the torture and murder of a child. But its main agenda is our complicity in such events through our prurient interest in the media they feed, and the way in which the media nourishes our private fantasies.

The anti-hero of the piece is K. D. Dufford – a solitary, unappetising, out of work warehouse hand from the West Riding of Yorkshire. His plan is to murder a child in order to leave his 'mark' on the world. He has just visited the flat of Ellen and Keith Lubb and been introduced to their ten-year-old daughter, his intended victim.

Ellen Lubb is thirty-one. She is described as 'comfortably covered, dowdy and homely'. This scene is her fantasy version of that first meeting with Dufford where we are eavesdropping on her thoughts as she dusts the flat. The dialogue is written in heavy Yorkshire dialect. Notice there is no punctuation, as her thoughts come tumbling out: We hear her aspirations for a sweeter, more aesthetic life expressed in the heightened language of cheap romantic fiction, the kind of books a woman like Ellen might read. Look how that contrasts with the language she uses about her 'slob' husband Keith, his 'lying' friend Thagney and her 'mucky' job. While Lubb and Thagney 'guzzle', Dufford is presented as a lyrical boyish hero. The images are almost filmic – Ellen's romantic version of events moving in and out of focus with her dismal reality in a stream of consciousness that we enter and exit mid-thought.

Think how Ellen's 'candle-lit, bare-shouldered' version of herself might affect her demeanour and the way she moves and speaks while dusting. By the end of the speech a director

might consider bathing the scene in rosy light and cueing
the wind machine!

———————

The Lubbs' Flat. **Ellen** *is dusting round the furniture. We hear her
thoughts.*

Ellen on'y an instant it was but right in t' me eyes like pale jools
like when 'e sed 'allo like right polite an' not like slob Lubb but like
right gentle an' not like Thagney's lies which Lubb drinks in an'
gives 'im ev'rything so I 'ave t' type in that mucky sausage skin
fact'ry which is not right for me not wine not candles not bare
shoulders as A shud be inspirin' like a great artist or doctor an' be
like right complex an' sensitive A sacrificed all that when 'e forced
me t' marry an' if it wasn't for me darlin' Janet well it's no use
wishin' this's like my penance an' life is sufferin' Keith knows that
an' when we spoke like at t' same moment an' 'e sed go on right
considerate an' as A spoke A felt 'is sorta gaze on me not undressin'
but right appreciative an' A sed wud y' like sum coffy an' 'e didn't
say yes like they did just after a guzzle but 'ad t' be pressed an' 'e
sorta gave a little like laff right boyish like right winsome an' like
right spontaneous an' 'is eyes sparkled an 'is voice sed right luvly
an' gentle

Lubb *enters, dressed in his drab outdoor jacket and with a lot of reading
matter under his arm. He doesn't look at her. She watches him out of the
corner of her eye. He plonks the reading matter down, goes to the
television set, switches it on. Light comes up, we can't hear any sound,*
Lubb *sits watching it intently.*

wot a contrast wi' Keith when A came back wi' t' coffy 'e stood up so
sprightly an' right light limbed like right slim an' nimble like a yung
deer an' 'e faced me with 'is fair skin an' t' breeze like caught 'is
right gentle fair 'air an' we

Black out.

Plenty *by David Hare*

This play was first produced to great acclaim in 1978. The action spans two decades of Susan Traherne's life. It charts the decline of her mental health against the changing social and political landscape of Britain, from post-war austerity to the 'you've never had it so good' plenty of the 1950s and '60s. The twelve scenes are not arranged chronologically, but home in on a random series of snapshots from Susan's life. It begins with a passionate, life-changing encounter with a British parachutist in occupied France during the war, when Susan was a courier for the Resistance.

This scene is set in 1956 at the time of the Suez crisis. Susan is in her mid-thirties. Compared to the heightened experiences of the war, everything since seems immoral and shallow. She has found it impossible to move on. After working in thankless jobs in shipping and advertising, she has suffered depression and a mental breakdown. She has been 'rescued' by Raymond Brock, a stuffy career diplomat she met in Brussels after the war.

In this scene she has been married to Raymond for some years. They are hosting a small diplomatic gathering in their opulent home. But the role of diplomat's wife does not sit easily with Susan. In spite of the importance of the event, Susan has been behaving inappropriately all evening, publicly sniping at her long-suffering husband, challenging his Foreign Office boss on the Government's stance on Suez, pushing the limits of civilised behaviour, and causing everyone acute embarrassment. She is either drunk or on medication, being described in the stage directions as 'dangerously cheerful'. In order to diffuse the tension, Brock encourages one of his guests to talk about a Bergman film she has seen. Susan, however, will not be halted, and in the pause left by everyone's embarrassment she continues her outburst, careless of the pain she is causing.

The beginning of the speech is bright and brittle having the form of a polite exchange but with a destructive subtext. Her seemingly civil, 'Is it getting a bit chilly in here?' refers as much to the atmosphere she has created as to the weather. Britain's recent engagement in war in Egypt, which she finds self-interested and immoral, triggers recollections of her own intense wartime experiences. The tension of the situation, grief at the loss of those times and disillusionment with the present engulfs her. Tears flood down her cheeks until she is barely able to speak.

It is her husband she targets towards the end of the speech, cruelly comparing her sterile life with him with her passionate wartime encounter. It's hurtful and very public, but Susan is too emotionally charged to care.

I've tacked on the speech from the end of the Act. Here Susan regains her brittle composure and engages in heavy irony about the political situation and the physical 'plenty' of her life that contrasts so starkly with the emotional vacuum inside.

Susan Is it getting a little bit chilly in here? October nights. Those poor parachutists. I do know how they feel. Even now. Cities. Fields. Trees. Farms. Dark spaces. Lights. The parachute opens. We descend.

Pause.

Of course we were comparatively welcome, not always ecstatic, not the Gaullists of course, but by and large we did make it our business to land in countries where we were wanted. Certainly the men were. I mean, some of the relationships, I can't tell you. I remember a colleague telling me of the heat, of the smell of a particular young girl, the hot wet smell he said. Nothing since. Nothing since then. I can't see the Egyptian girls somehow . . . no. Not in Egypt now. I mean there were broken hearts when we left. I mean, there are girls today who mourn Englishmen who died in Dachau, died naked in Dachau, men with whom they had spent a single night. Well.

Pause. The tears are pouring down **Susan**'s *face, she can barely speak.*

But then . . . even for myself I do like to make a point of sleeping with men I don't know. I do find once you get to know them you usually don't want to sleep with them any more . . .

Brock *gets up and shouts at the top of his voice across the room.*

68

[**Brock** *Please can you stop, can you stop fucking talking for five fucking minutes on end?*

Susan *I would stop, I would stop, I would stop fucking talking if I ever heard anyone else say anything worth fucking stopping talking for.*

Pause. Then **Darwin** moves.

Darwin *I'm sorry. I apologize. I really must go.*

He crosses the room.

M. Wong. Farewell.

Wong *We are behind you sir. There is wisdom in your expedition.*

Darwin *Thank you.*

Wong *May I say sir, these gyps need whipping and you are the man to do it.*

Darwin *Thank you very much. Mme Wong.*

Mme Wong *We never really met.*

Darwin *No. No. We never met, that is true. But perhaps before I go, I may nevertheless set you right on a point of fact. Ingmar Bergman is not a bloody Norwegian, he is a bloody Swede.* (He nods slightly.) *Good night everyone.*

Darwin goes out. Brock gets up and goes to the door, then turns.]

Susan Isn't this an exciting week? Don't you think? Isn't this thrilling? Don't you think? Everything is up for grabs. At last. We will see some changes. Thank the Lord.

Now, there was dinner. I made some more dinner for Leonard. A little ham. And chicken. And some pickles and tomato. And lettuce. And there are a couple of pheasants in the fridge. And I can get twelve bottles of claret from the cellar. Why not?

There is plenty.

Shall we eat again?

Play with a Tiger *by Doris Lessing*

This play was first produced at the Comedy Theatre in 1962. It is about the battle of the sexes and is set in the emergent postwar, classless society of 1958. Lessing, one of the first writers to put women's issues at the heart of her work, describes it as 'a play about rootless, 'declassed' people who live in bed sitting rooms or the cheaper hotel rooms . . .'

The action takes place over one long night in the life of Australian ex pat, Anna Freeman. Anna is thirty-five and works on the 'artistic fringes' as a writer in inner city London. She is a widow with a young son, and is clever, sexually attractive and self-sufficient. But she is at the bottom: lonely, vulnerable and desperately wanting a committed relationship. She loves Dave, a mercurial, slightly younger American, who is promiscuous and 'rootless on principle'. In spite of their feelings, they are temperamentally unsuited to marriage because neither is prepared to conform to society's rules and stereotypes, or make the necessary compromises for their relationship to work.

This speech comes quite near the end of the play. Dave has just come back into Anna's life after weeks of typically unexplained absence. He has only been back a few hours and it has been a long night. Unknown to him, Anna has recently discovered that he had got Janet Stevens, a very conventional young American woman, pregnant. Dave doesn't yet know about the baby, or that Anna knows about this relationship. It is a card she has up her sleeve and is just about to play.

Just prior to this speech, she has just given Dave his marching orders. She's hurting: if he really wants an 'open' relationship with a free, independent woman, what is he doing getting trapped by conventional little Janet Stevens? Utterly miserable, she stares out of her window at the world below her flat. She watches a man who has spent the night lurking outside a neighbouring brothel. The streets are peopled with the lawless and the dispossessed. Couples cling together to keep the dark out. It's a savage lonely world out there. The speech expresses Jane's longing for the

safe and simple life expressed in 'we must love one another',
but she mocks its implausibility and her desire for it even as
it comes out of her mouth.

————————————

Anna (*in pain*) Dave, you have no right, you have no right . . .
you're a very careless person, Dave . . . (*She gets off the bed and goes to
the window.*) What's the use of talking of rights and wrongs? Or of
right or wrong? O.K., it's a jungle. Anything goes. I should have let
myself get pregnant. One catches a man by getting pregnant. People
like you and me make life too complicated. Back to reality. (*Looking
down.*) My God, that poor fool is still down there.

[*Dave Anna, don't freeze up on me.*]

Anna You want to know what I've been doing? Well, I've been
standing here at night looking into the street and trying not to
think about what you've been doing. I've been standing here. At
about eleven at night the law and the order dissolve. The girls stand
at their window there, kissing or quarrelling as the case might be, in
between customers. The wolves prowl along the street. Gangs of
kids rush by, living in some frightened lonely violent world that
they think we don't understand – ha! So they think we don't
understand what's driving them crazy? Old people living alone go
creeping home, alone. The women who live alone, after an hour of
talking to strangers in a pub, go home, alone. And sometimes a
married couple or lovers – and they can't wait to get inside, behind
the walls, they can't wait to lock the doors against this terrible city.
And they're right.

[*Dave They're not right.*]

Anna Put your arms around one other human being, and let the
rest of the world go hang – the world is terrifying, so shut it out.
That's what people are doing everywhere, and perhaps they are
right.

[*Dave Anna, say it!*

Anna All right.] You're an egotist, and egotists can never bear the thought of a new generation. That's all. And I'm an egotist and what I call my self-respect is more important to me than anything else. And that's all. There's nothing new in it. There's nothing new anywhere. I shall die of boredom. Sometimes at night I look out into a street and I imagine that somewhere is a quiet room, and in the room is a man or a woman, thinking. And quite soon there will be a small new book – a book of one page perhaps, and on the page one small new thought. And we'll all read it and shout: Yes, yes, that's it.

[*Dave Such as?*]

Anna (*mocking*) We must love one another or die, something new like that.

The Maids *by Jean Genet*
(translated by Bernard Frechtman)

The Maids is an erotically-charged drama about subservience
and domination in the master-servant relationship.

Solange and Claire Lemercier are two sisters in their early
thirties who are employed as maids in the household of a
vain young mistress. Their love-hate relationship with
Madame is expressed in role-plays in which they improvise
her murder, taking it in turns to impersonate her. But the
fatal end to the fantasy is always interrupted by their
mistress' return. The edge of their fantasy frequently blurs
with reality as erotic tensions and a jealous power struggle
between the sisters is played out.

The maids attempt to keep Madame for themselves by
fabricating evidence against her lover and 'informing' on
him to the police. But to their alarm, the lover is released
without charge. Fearing discovery, the sisters decide to
actually kill their mistress by poisoning her tea. Their plot
comes unstuck, however, when Madame fails to drink it.
While Madame goes to meet her lover, Claire clothes herself
in her mistress' white dress and the sisters play another of
their ritual killing games. This time they short-circuit the
preliminaries and the game appears to reach its dénouement.

In this scene, alone and unobserved Solange fantasises
about strangling Claire in the kitchen. Or has she actually
done it? Initially it's unclear. The identities of the real
Madame and Claire's impersonation are confused. The
speech gains energy as Solange engrosses herself in a series
of grotesque scenarios in which she plays all the characters
in several empowering versions of herself. It's a hybrid of
madness and nightmare, and like a dream it shifts between
locations, identities and tenses, flipping backwards and
forwards in time and changing tack as fast as thought. The
dislocated scenes project Solange's emotional conflicts
about her relationship with both her mistress and sister.
They are expressions of how she would like things to be.
They enable her to climb out of her hated subservience and
become the heroine of her own life. Look how she has the
upper hand in all her manifestations, whether she is

speaking patronisingly to her employer, flouting the police, or nobly mounting the scaffold in her incarnation as 'Mademoiselle Solange, the famous criminal'. The speech is driven by Solange's subconscious resentments and desires. Like the subconscious, it has an inexorable life of its own and it should carry the audience along on its powerful and unpredictable tide.

The play ends with an ironic and triumphal reversal of the first scene, when Claire drinks the poison prepared for her mistress and dies.

Solange Madame. . . . At last! Madame is dead! . . . laid out on the linoleum . . . strangled by the dish-gloves. What? Oh, Madame may remain seated. . . . Madame may call me Mademoiselle Solange. . . . Exactly. It's because of what I've done. Madame and Monsieur will call me Mademoiselle Solange Lemercier. . . . Madame should have taken off that black dress. It's grotesque. (*She imitates Madame's voice.*) So I'm reduced to wearing mourning for my maid. As I left the cemetery all the servants of the neighbourhood marched past me as if I were a member of the family. I've so often been part of the family. Death will see the joke through to the bitter end. . . . What? Oh! Madame needn't feel sorry for me. I'm Madame's equal and I hold my head high. . . . Oh! And there are things Monsieur doesn't realize. He doesn't know that he used to obey our orders. (*She laughs.*) Ah! Ah! Monsieur was a tiny little boy. Monsieur toed the line when we threatened. No, Inspector, no. . . . I won't talk! I won't say a word. I refuse to speak about our complicity in this murder. . . . The dresses? Oh, Madame could have kept them. My sister and I had our own. Those we used to put on at night, in secret. Now, I have my own dress, and I'm your equal. I wear the red garb of criminals. Monsieur's laughing at me? He's smiling at me. Monsieur thinks I'm mad. He's thinking maids should have better taste than to make gestures reserved for Madame! Monsieur really forgives me? Monsieur is the soul of kindness. He'd like to vie with me in grandeur. But I've scaled the fiercest heights. Madame now sees my

loneliness – at last! Yes, I am alone. And fearsome. I might say cruel
things, but I can be kind. . . . Madame will get over her fright. She'll
get over it well enough. What with her flowers and perfumes and
gowns and jewels and lovers. As for me, I've my sister. . . . Yes. I dare
speak of these things. I do, Madame. There's nothing I won't dare.
And who could silence me, who? Who would be so bold as to say to
me: 'My dear child!' I've been a servant. Well and good. I've made
the gestures a servant must make. I've smiled at Madame. I've bent
down to make the bed, bent down to scrub the tiles, bent down to
peel vegetables, to listen at doors, to glue my eye to keyholes! But
now I stand upright. And firm. I'm the strangler. Mademoiselle
Solange, the one who strangled her sister! . . . Me be still? Madame
is delicate, really. But I pity Madame. I pity Madame's whiteness,
her satiny skin, and her little ears, and little wrists. . . . Eh? I'm the
black crow. . . . Oh! Oh! I have my judges. I belong to the police.
Claire? She was really very fond of Madame. . . . YOUR dresses
again! And THAT white dress, THAT one, which I forbade her to put
on, the one you wore the night of the Opera Ball, the night you
poked fun at her, because she was sitting in the kitchen admiring a
photo of Gary Cooper. . . . Madame will remember. Madame will
remember her gentle irony, the maternal grace with which she took
the magazine from us, and smiled. Nor will Madame forget that she
called her Clarinette. Monsieur laughed until the tears rolled down
his cheeks. . . . Eh? Who am I? The monstrous soul of servantdom!
. . . No, Inspector, I'll explain nothing in their presence. That's *our*
business. It would be a fine thing if masters could pierce the
shadows where servants live. . . . That, my child, is our darkness,
ours. (*She lights a cigarette, and smokes clumsily. The smoke makes her
cough.*) Neither you nor anyone else will be told anything. Just tell
yourselves that this time Solange has gone through with it. . . . You
see her dressed in red. She is going out. (*She goes to the window, opens
it, and steps out on the balcony. Facing the night, with her back to the
audience, she delivers the following speech. A slight breeze makes the
curtains stir.*) Going out. Descending the great stairway.
Accompanied by the police. Out on your balconies to see her
making her way among the shadowy penitents! It's noon. She's

carrying a nine-pound torch. The hangman follows close behind. He's whispering sweet nothings in her ear. Claire! The hangman's by my side! Now take your hand off my waist. He's trying to kiss me! Let go of me! Ah! Ah! (*She laughs.*) The hangman's trifling with me. She will be led in procession by all the maids of the neighbourhood, by all the servants who accompanied Claire to her final resting place. They'll all be wearing crowns, flowers, streamers, banners. They'll toll the bell. The funeral will unfold its pomp. It's beautiful, isn't it? First come the butlers, in full livery, but without silk lining. They're wearing their crowns. Then come the footmen, the lackeys in knee breeches and white stockings. They're wearing their crowns. Then come the valets, and then the chambermaids wearing our colours. Then the porters. And then come the delegations from heaven. And I'm leading them. The hangman's lulling me. I'm being acclaimed. I'm pale and I'm about to die. . . . (*She returns to the room.*) And what flowers! They gave her such a lovely funeral, didn't they? Oh! Claire, poor little Claire! (*She bursts into tears and collapses into an armchair.*) What? (*She gets up.*) It's no use, Madame, I'm obeying the police. They're the only ones who understand me. They too belong to the world of outcasts, the world you touch only with tongs.

Visible only to the audience, Claire, during the last few moments, has been leaning with her elbows against the jamb of the kitchen door and listening to her sister.

Now we are Mademoiselle Solange Lemercier, that Lemercier woman. The famous criminal. And above all, Monsieur need not be uneasy. I'm not a maid. I have a noble soul. . . . (*She shrugs her shoulders.*) No, no, not another word, my dear fellow. Ah; Madame's not forgetting what I've done for her. . . . No, no, she must not forget my devotion. . . .

Meanwhile Claire enters through the door at the left. She is wearing the white dress.

And in spite of my forbidding it, Madame continues to stroll about the apartment. She will please sit down . . . and listen to me. . . . (*To Claire.*) Claire . . . we're raving!

What Shall I Wear? *by Hermione Gingold*

Actress and writer Hermione Gingold died in 1987. She was a legend in her own lifetime. By the Second World War she had become a huge star with almost iconic status, packing the West End with performances in popular revues.

The revue is an outdated theatrical form that went out of fashion in the 1960s. It was a hybrid sort of entertainment, consisting of quick sketches, monologues and songs, usually with a topical satirical flavour.

This monologue is taken from the *Sweet and Low* revue, which was a huge success and ran for 264 performances at the Ambassadors Theatre in 1943. You can just imagine the relief provided by such evenings during The Second World War. These were days when actors were expected to sound upper-middle class and played to audiences of the same ilk. Not a kitchen sink in sight! Going to the theatre was a social occasion. You dressed to the nines and dined afterwards. This is the world occupied by our character and the audience whom she addresses directly.

Hermione Gingold once said, 'I don't try to be funny dear, I just have a certain slant on life.' It's a good note for this and most other comedy. Find the character and the comedy will play itself. In this case, the character can be young or old. You can really make this monologue your own, but remember it is very much a period piece. Although its satirical edge will probably be lost today, it is not difficult to identify with a character preoccupied with the niceties of fashion and good food while Europe burns and England pulls in its belt. Lip-service is paid to war-time austerity with her bracketed references to dried eggs and tinned fruit, but she is clearly from that 'born to rule' class that built the Empire. Poor thing, it's dreadful to have to wear last year's fashion and have to 'make do'. The spirit of everything that made England great – good clothes, bridge, fine tea and top cuisine – is what's at stake here. Stiff upper lip. Looking on the bright side. Maintaining standards. It's all very 'trying' but it *is* war-time and sometimes the only time you can get a good lunch is by licking the food-stains on your haute couture!

What shall I wear? What shall I wear? Which of us has not at some time or other, during these trying days, been faced with this difficult problem?

You rush to the wardrobe – and what do you find? Your last year's flank musquash has been all but eaten by a moth – your beige crepe-de-soie has a large tear just below the inverted pleat, which gives fullness and swing to an otherwise plain tailored skirt.

Ah, a thought strikes you – what about my *marron* two-piece with the sweet-pea reverse? You detach it delicately from its hanger – what do you see? Horror, devastation! For on the third tuck from the right, just where the bishop sleeve cleverly meets the blouse, you see a large stain – it resembles in shape the isle of Ceylon. (Ceylon is a pear-shaped island at the foot of India, population 3,000, chief export tea – that is by the way.) What can it be, you ask yourself? Tea, coffee, cocoa, custard (made with dried eggs), fruit (tinned of course) or austerity trifle, for until you know what sort of stain it is, you cannot remove it. You raise it to your lips – umm . . . mulligatawny soup, delicious . . .! Regretfully you put it aside and look at the skirt – except for the back, which is seated and shiny, it looks as good as new. Why not wear the skirt with your bridge coat? Why not? I tell you why not, because even if we are at war, there is no reason why any self-respecting Englishwoman should wear a bridge coat unless she is definitely going to play bridge. Put it back, put it back, and you will feel you have done something to keep alive the spirit that went to build our empire.

Ah, but what is this? Your turquoise-blue knitted three-piece. You slip it on – ah, but what is that? On the very front a large triangular stain surrounded by four or five smaller ones.

Undaunted, you turn it back to front – it gives a most peculiar effect. No, you must remove the offending stains. Looking at them closely, you find tiny dried segments of . . . what? You raise the offending garment to your lips, a taste leaves no further doubt – fish cakes, your favourite dish, but perhaps a little tasteless without some kind of savoury sauce, be it piquant or tartare. Hastily, you hunt through your wardrobe and there, on the bust of your white satin evening dress, is a generous patch of anchovy sauce! Ah, but that makes all the difference in the world. But it leaves us with the clothing problem still unsolved, though you find the hard work has given you quite an appetite. Still, we mustn't give in, must we? That's not the spirit that got us out of the Black Hole of Calcutta, no! So we go on, blouse after blouse, dress after dress, stain after stain . . . salmon mayonnaise, ice cream, lobster salad, hock, jam sponge *à la crème, jugged hare,* coupe marron, smoked haddock and eggs, banana royal, potted shrimps, plum pudding with brandy butter. At last, at last, the garments are carefully sorted out for cleaning.

You may think regretfully as you look at them that you still have nothing to wear – but cheer up, for you must admit you've had a very good lunch!

The Bitter Tears of Petra Von Kant
by Rainer Werner Fassbinder
(translated by Anthony Vivas)

The Bitter Tears of Petra Von Kant is a charged drama about
sexual passion and possessive love. It is set in Germany in
the early 1970s.

Petra Von Kant is an ambitious woman in her mid-
thirties. She is a successful fashion designer and has become
both rich and a bit of a celebrity. She is middle-class,
liberated, independent, emotional, domineering and callous.
Petra's marriage to husband number two has recently fallen
apart and she is suing for divorce. Her friend Sidonie, who
has just returned to Germany after a long trip, has read in
the papers of Petra's marriage difficulties and has come
round to commiserate and share intimacies about men. The
friends are talking over morning coffee.

In this speech Petra is explaining to Sidonie why her
marriage failed. Her tone is dismissive and bitter. Everything about her husband disgusts her now: the way he eats,
the way he drinks, the way he smokes cigarettes. Her love is
dead and there is nothing left in the marriage to salvage.
She blames the failure of her relationship on her husband's
inability to handle her success and escape his gender
stereotype – something that was a hot topic of the period.
She takes no responsibility for herself.

She charts the journey of the relationship from his subtle
strategies to dominate, through his economic and emotional
loss of control, to more brutal methods of possessing her. The
fact that she allowed him to dominate her sexually long after
her love had died fills her with horror. But it is the shift from
the particular to the general that is the most telling aspect of
this speech. Look at the words she uses – revolting, filthy,
stink, nausea, howling, shame – and her shocking description of non-consensual sex. She judges all men by the
behaviour of one and it is Petra's deep antipathy to men that
drives the speech. Petra is ripe for what follows – a consuming
and needy passion for a beautiful much younger woman.

Petra Men! And their vanity! Oh, Sidonie. He wanted to pamper me, look after me. Oh yes, he took his role very seriously, he certainly allowed me an opinion, *but* – he was the breadwinner. And that way repression comes in through the back door. It goes like this: I take your point, I'm with you all the way, but . . . who earns the money, who slogs his guts out? So I couldn't win either way! Oh, darling. At first it was: Look, love, the money *you* earn goes straight into a deposit account, and in time we can treat ourselves to something special – a little cottage of our own, or a sports car or something. I just nodded, went along with it, because . . . he was so gentle, Sidonie, and sometimes the love he radiated all round him swept me off my feet and left me . . . breathless with happiness. Then his business crashed and at first, you know, it was almost funny seeing his stupid pride injured and if I'm honest I rather enjoyed it, especially because I really believed he'd see for himself how stupidly he was behaving. But he never did. Then later, when I tried to explain, tried to tell him it made no difference to me whether a man happens to be 'on top' or not, it was already too late. Whenever I touched on the subject – a stone wall came down, Sidonie, a solid stone wall. And then, bit by bit, all the openness started to die. I think I'd been fooling myself about him, and about us, and so I stopped. Stopped loving him. The last six months were terrible, Sidonie, terrible! Obviously he knew it was over, or at least sensed it. But he wouldn't *accept* it, oh no! Even by that stage he hadn't cottoned on. Knowing he couldn't have the real *me*, he tried to have me in bed. That's what I found so revolting. He tried technique, then force. I let him hold me down. I took it all. But . . . he just seemed so filthy.

[*Sidonie Petra!*]

Petra He stank! He stank of man. As only men can stink. What had once aroused me . . . now just filled me with nausea, and brought tears to my eyes. And when he mounted me . . .

[*Sidonie No, Petra! Please!*]

Petra Now I've started, kindly hear me out. He took me like a bull takes its cow. Not a glimmer of respect left, not a thought for my pleasure as a woman. The pain, Sidonie, you'd never dream it could hurt so much. And when sometimes in spite of myself I did . . . the shame! The shame. I felt so ashamed. He thought I was howling with pleasure, gratitude. He was so stupid, so stupid. Men are so bloody stupid.

Mary Barnes *by David Edgar*

This play is based on Dr Joseph Berke's book, *A Journey into Madness*, and explores the true story of schizophrenic artist and writer Mary Barnes, who spent much of her life struggling against and documenting her illness in words and painting.

The play is set in the 1960s in a therapeutic community that provides an alternative environment for the mentally ill. It addresses the nature and treatment of madness. It was first performed at the Birmingham Repertory Theatre in 1978.

Mary is a schizophrenic in her early forties. She is a devout Catholic whose painting is rooted in religious imagery. David Edgar describes the real Mary Barnes as 'passionate, intense, demanding and self-obsessed', a description which certainly fits the character here. Mary's early life has been spent in conventional mental hospitals. Now she has a place in the therapeutic community, where she has been living for some time. In spite of their more liberal regime, her behaviour has become increasingly difficult to deal with. She has refused food, regressed to babyhood, assaulted staff and inmates, and smeared herself and the walls with excrement. As part of a fragile road to recovery, she has been encouraged to paint pictures. These have a powerful religious content and through them she has found a mechanism for expressing things for which she can't find words.

In this scene she is drawing a picture of the Crucifixion. Totally absorbed, she tries to articulate the sense of separation, absence and fragmentation she felt as a child, identifying, as she draws, with Christ's suffering. She plays all the characters in her picture: soldiers, dragging Christ up the hill, pushing and bullying; Christ himself, dragging heavy feet and 'clump, clumping' to the hilltop, like her 'all clumpy, weary', and the soldiers passing the hammer and hammering the nails. The exchanges are simplistic and expressed in the language of a child's story–book. The robbers crucified with Christ haggle with him about which one will go to heaven. Christ drinks the vinegar on a sponge that is offered to him like a child being offered a spoonful of food. 'No, no. The sky's gone crimson' is a cry from the heart and, like Christ's cry to God to save him – 'God, my

God, why have you [forsaken me]' – has roots in Mary's own feelings of abandonment. The bomb she describes is the agony inside her. It is the tearing pain with which she identifies and which she is trying to work through and express in her drawing of Christ's agony.

Research into the true story of Mary Barnes and the nature of schizophrenia will be very helpful when you are trying to unpick this difficult piece.

Mary Remember, as a child, strange feelings. Feel apart. Not here, not anywhere, a thing. All clumpy, weary. Head all big and fuzzy. Bits of me.

Pause. She picks up a crayon. Starts to draw. Then she suddenly starts talking, playing people in the drawing.

Hey. You.

Hey, get a move on.
Heavy.
Hey, you come on. Move.
It's heavy, clumping up the hill. Like feet in treacle. Mustn't fall.
Come on. Don't whine. We haven't got all day.
Clump clump. Clump clump. We're there.
The top. The silver sky.

All right then, pass the hammer.
One. Two. THREE.

Long pause. **Mary** *still.*

I'm blown apart. There's bits of me.
All floating to the other side. A leg, an arm. I'm on the moon.
Another.

Pause. She starts to draw again.

Hey, you.
Who, me?

You don't know what you're doing.
Listen, what he says. We don't know what we're doing!
Hur hur hur.
Hey, you.
Who me?
I'm telling you. Today, you're going to heaven. One of you.
Oh, yuh? Big deal. Which one? Hur hur.
Hey, you.
Who, me?
I'm thirsty.

Drink it up, then. Like a good boy.
Drink it up.

No, no. The sky's gone crimson.
God oh God why have you . . .

Long pause. **Mary** *still.*

And the urge to spew it out, the bomb. But more you tear at it, the more it seems to cling, to stick inside you. Got to lie with it, and work it through.

Pause. She starts to draw again.

Hey, you!
You up there. Come down.
If you're so great, so clever, come on down.
He can't.
Well, ask him why. Can whisper.
Can't. Can't talk.
He's sulking, in a paddy. Cos he can't come down.
I won't.
I won't come down.
Stay in the dark.

Pause.

Be empty. Nothing. Void. Hang on.

The Rehearsal *by Jean Anouilh*
(translated by Jeremy Sams)

This is a stylish play about the corruption of innocence. It takes place over three days while a decadent aristocratic couple and their house guests rehearse a play by Marivaux in full Louise XV costume for an evening entertainment. It is set in 1950s France.

The Count and Countess have inherited 'Ferbroques', an eighteenth-century chateau willed to them by the Countess' aunt. But a whimsical condition attached to their inheritance stipulates that twelve orphans must be brought up in the west wing. In order to comply, the couple employs Lucile, the impecunious goddaughter of Monsieur Damiens, their solicitor. While they continue their pleasure seeking lives, she is charged with looking after the children.

The Count – Tiger – and Countess take lovers as they please, but when the Countess realises her husband has genuinely fallen in love with the innocent Lucile, she colludes with the Count's current mistress to destroy the relationship and drive Lucile from the house. Unknown to the Countess, Lucile returns the Count's feelings and they have consummated their love.

The Countess plants an expensive emerald ring in Lucile's room in the hope that the shame of being accused of theft will drive her away. But the Count thwarts their plans. At this point in the play he has forced the Countess to swallow her malice, to apologise and ask Lucile to stay. The difference in the women is highlighted when Lucile naively asks the Countess if she loves her husband and thinks having fun all the time makes the Count happy. The Countess is a scheming, dangerous and manipulative woman who has been out-manoeuvred by her husband and humiliated into apologising. She is incensed but has no option but to comply.

From the first sentence of the speech the Countess pulls age and rank, refusing to be drawn into any intimate exchange with a social inferior. She has been pushed into a corner. Her cosy way of life is in jeopardy and she will use every tactic she can muster to protect her corner. She appears relaxed, urbane and sincere, the older, wiser woman with Lucile's best interests at heart. But behind the caring, almost motherly façade a calculating mind is at work. Her cynical, carefully worded attempts to warn Lucile off having a relationship with the Count, pair her off with her amorous godfather and buy her off with the emerald ring speak volumes about the shallow, sterile world she inhabits. It is a world in which Lucile's idealism about love has no place and will finally be destroyed.

_____

Countess My dear young lady, if we are going to have this conversation, and it seems that we must, you will forgive me if I do not allow it to assume too personal a tone. I loathe personal questions. Tiger wants me to ask you to stay – so I'm asking you. He'll have a fit if we have to cancel the performance. Anyway, why leave? We all admire your considerable efforts on behalf of those poor children and we certainly have no particular reason to prolong our stay in 'Ferbroques'. Tiger gets bored witless in the country. Once the party's over, we'll be whizzing back to Paris for the season. Then everything will be just as it was, won't it? So let's part friends, shall we? And once again, do please forgive that little episode. Tiger's quite capable of going into a sulk – for anything up to a week. And he would, if he thought you bore me any sort of grudge. We hardly know each other of course, but you must be aware of how much I value your godfather, M. Damiens. *A propos*, we were talking about you only this morning. You know he has an enormous affection for you?

[*Lucile Yes, he has told me.*]

Countess A man, I can't help feeling, who has had his fair share of suffering. He's lived apart from his wife for some years now, hasn't he? And she doesn't seem in their married life, how shall I put it, to have afforded him all the attention he might have deserved. Behind a rather forbidding exterior, he's actually a man of surprising sensitivity. Yes, he talked about you at some length.

[*Lucile Really?*

Countess Yes, really.] My child, I did get a little bit irritated just now, I'll admit it. All things considered, I'm really very fond of you. You're so young. You have this disarming way of seeming to know everything. But I'm sure that deep down under that Quaker seriousness, there's a doomed little moth dying to singe its wings in the first flame it can find. You think . . . oh, yes, it will be gorgeous . . . it will be everything you've ever dreamed of . . . So you live out the dream for a week, perhaps two. Then your eyes open. Wide open and weeping. Damiens told me that you were proud; proud and poor. A great quality coupled with a great disadvantage. Of course, you may well meet someone from your own walk of life. But that won't last all that long either. The Prince Charming of the Young Farmers' Ball – blushing – picking you violets. I'll give him two years to turn into a sulky, petty-minded little tyrant. You're worth much more than that. It's always a great temptation for a girl just to go mad. But, believe me, the temptation to be totally sane is just as great and twice as dangerous. If you're pretty, intelligent and penniless, let's face it, you'll always be a bit declassé. You have to take what you can. Damiens, who is a friend of mine, and I were very worried about you this morning. (*A beat. She gets up. Wanders nonchalantly to a table.*) Briefly, it's like this. His wife is barking mad, of course, and lives out in the country. She's ill. She's older than he is. She won't live long. Damiens is a man of honour and still very handsome. I remember fifteen or twenty years ago when he used to come to visit my mother – I wonder if I should be telling you all this? Of course I was just a girl, but I was madly in love with him for a whole winter . . . At least think about it. I'm talking to you as a woman who understands life, who is quite a bit older than you and who would be unhappy, really unhappy to see you squandering your youth on some mad escapade that has no future. When you have no status, when you're alone in the world, you have to look to the future. My God, I know it's no fun. It's not what you expect or want when you're twenty. But it's the way of the world, my dear. And there's not much either of us can do about it. (*A pause. She looks at* **Lucile**.) Listen to me, Damiens has served us so faithfully, and for such a long time. As far as I am concerned, you would be as good as his wife. This emerald will be my wedding present to you. (*Offering it.*)

What Shall We Tell Caroline?
by John Mortimer

This one-act play is set in the dilapidated living room of
Highland Close School, a small boarding school for boys.
Arthur Loudon is the irascible Headmaster who, with his
wife Lily, is preparing an eighteenth birthday celebration
for their daughter, Caroline. She hasn't spoken a word to
either of them for some time. They feel they should offer
advice for her coming of age and pass on some of their
experience.

Lily is middle-aged. She is described in the stage directions as an 'untidy woman, once inconspicuously good
looking, whose face now wears an expression of puzzled
contentment'. The play is set in the late fifties, but Lily
significantly wears a feminine evening dress of the pre-war
thirties. Since her marriage to Arthur she has been treated as
'one of the chaps'. Her husband's nickname for her, 'Bin',
defines her identity and how he wants to see her as a
'thoroughly good chap'. Life is made tolerable by innocent
flirtations with the debonair, if balding, Tony, the only
other teacher at the school. Tony's admiration, imaginative
games and musical evenings make Lily feel romantic and
womanly. She believes Tony loves her. She certainly loves
him.

The men quarrel over Lily all the time and Arthur never
misses an opportunity to snipe and argue about almost
everything – the date of the Spanish Armada, the exact
position of Gibraltar. But an argument about what advice to
give Caroline crystallises their different attitudes to life.
Arthur maintains that Caroline should be told about the
responsibilities of adulthood, about 'running a school,
getting married . . .' Maybe she might even be permitted a
glass of beer! Tony moots that when Caroline grows older it
won't be her mistakes she regrets!

In this scene where Lily finds herself alone with her
daughter, she realises she has her own advice to impart that
perhaps only Tony would understand. Kneeling at her silent
daughter's feet, she describes how her life has been incre-
mentally subsumed by her desiccating role as 'headmaster's

wife'. She relates how difficult she has found it to deny her womanly impulses in order to be the 'good chap' she was expected to be by her family and Arthur; to always be the responsible one, always a good sport, when she longed for champagne, femininity and romance. It is as if Caroline's silence and coming of age have given her permission to express a lifetime of longing and regret. Where has she gone wrong? She doesn't want her life to be a blueprint for Caroline's. Tony's romantic attentions have made her feel alive again – 'as if she was born to be a woman'. This is what it should be like. A mother is telling her daughter that the only thing that really matters is love.

Lily I'm a woman, Caroline. And you're going to be one as well. Nothing can stop you. I'm a woman and what does Arthur call me? He calls me Bin. Bin, when my name is Lily. Now does Bin sound like a woman's name to you? You know why he calls me Bin? Because he wants me to be his friend, his assistant, his colleague, his thoroughly good chap. To rough it with him on a walking tour through life. He's said that to me, Caroline. How can I be a good chap, I wasn't born a chap. *My sex gets in the way.* That's why he gets so angry. (*She gets up and moves about the room.*) Look Caroline, do you know why he calls me Bin? Because my father did and my uncle did and so did my five brothers who all married soft hearted tittering girls in fluffy pullovers which came off on them like falling hair and white peep toed shoes and had pet names for their hot water bottles. Those brothers called me Bin. Good old Bin, you can put her on the back of the motor bike. Bin's marvellous, she can go in the dicky because her hair's always in a tangle and her cheeks are like bricks and the wind can't do her any harm, but Babs or Topsy or Melanie has to sit in front because she's such a fuss pot and so I can change gear next to her baby pink and artificial silk and get her angora all tied up in my Harris tweed. If you take Bin out it's for great slopping pints and the other one about the honeymoon couple in the French hotel, and then you can be sick in the hedge on the way because Bin's a good chap. We're women Caroline. They buy us beer when we long to order protection and flattery and excitement and crème de menthe and little bottles of sparkling wine with silver paper tops and oh God, we long to be kept warm. Aren't I right? Isn't that how we feel? Mothers and daughters and wives. . . . (*Kneeling again.*) Oh Caroline tell me I'm right. Caroline. Speak to us. What have we done wrong?

Caroline *says nothing, but, for the first time she smiles slowly and puts her hands on her mother's shoulder.* **Lily** *gets up, gets the tray which she has left leaning against the wall and begins to stack the plates.*

Lily Anyway all my friends got married and there was only Arthur. He was small and violent and believed in everything. Life wasn't much fun at home, my brothers got married and their wives refused to take on their pets. After the youngest left I was walking out with five Alsatian dogs. Father economized on the wedding. 'We needn't hire a car for Bin,' he said. My brother Tommy took me to the church on the back of his motor bike. My first long dress and I was rushed up to my wedding wearing goggles and waving in the wind like a flag. We're women, Caroline. There's supposed to be a mystery about us. We should be sprung on our men like a small surprise in the warmth and darkness of the night – not delivered by a boy on a motor bike like a parcel that's come undone in the post. It shouldn't be like that for you Caroline. The day after the marriage I told Arthur I loved him. 'There are more important things than love,' he said. 'What more important things?' 'Companionship,' he said, 'helping one another. Now we're dedicated, our lives are dedicated.' 'What to?' I asked him. 'The boys.' Can you believe it? Those dreadful children coughing like old sheep upstairs. I was dedicated to *them*. I went to look at them. They were in striped pyjamas, they looked like little old convicts with cropped heads and match-stick arms and legs. They had hard, sexless voices and the faint, cold smell of lead pencils. And you know what? Arthur said it would make them think of me as more of a sport. He told them to call me Bin. I ask you. Is that a name for a woman?

The Night of the Iguana
by Tennessee Williams

This received its first performance in New York in 1961. It is
set in the summer of 1940 on the veranda of the dilapidated
Costa Verde hotel, on the West Coast of Mexico, where a
group of disparate characters come together by chance. Its
theme, in Tennessee William's own words, ' is how to live
beyond despair and still live.'

Hannah is a New England spinster who is pushing forty.
She is an itinerant, quick-sketch artist travelling with her
grandfather, Nonno – the world's 'oldest living and practising
poet.' They have been travelling the world for years. He is her
family. They pay their way by his recitations and her quick
sketches of tourists. Hannah is a subtle but smart operator, an
independent, resilient and resourceful lady. She is fastidious
and astringent, at times shy, restrained, but by no means
unattractive. She is a virgin with a natural reluctance towards
any kind of intimacy – a lonely woman who knows she has
no other resource but herself.

Hannah has befriended Shannon, a down and out ex-
priest who has been working as a tour guide, conducting
coachfuls of Baptist ladies round religious sites in his
capacity as 'a man of God'. Shannon has had a bad night.
The Tour Company has just discovered his shady history,
and that he conducted one of the ladies to dubious haunts
not on the itinerary. Consequently they have sacked him.
As a result Shannon has gone to pieces and has had to be
restrained. His crisis of faith and his despair are met with a
peculiar kind of faith in Hannah, who knows that human
beings really can find salvation in each other. She can relate
to what he is feeling and manages to calm him down with
quiet talk and herbal tea. When he is a little calmer, they
exchange intimacies on the veranda in the manner of
strangers who may never meet again.

In this speech Hannah describes how she conquered her
own 'dark night of the soul' and, through her painting,
found a light at the end of a dark tunnel. Salvation, she
maintains, comes from looking out of yourself, not in.

The end of the speech is the painful acknowledgement of

her grandfather's approaching death. Look how abruptly she changes the subject when she gets close to the raw emotion of that thought.

———————————

Hannah I never cracked up, I couldn't afford to. Of course, I nearly did once. I was young once, Mr Shannon, but I was one of those people who can be young without really having their youth, and not to have your youth when you are young is naturally very disturbing. But I was lucky. My work, this occupational therapy that I gave myself – painting and doing quick character sketches – made me look out of myself, not in, and gradually, at the far end of the tunnel that I was struggling out of I began to see this faint, very faint grey light – the light of the world outside me – and I kept climbing towards it. I had to.

[*Shannon Did it stay a grey light?*

Hannah No, no, it turned white.

Shannon Only white, never gold?

Hannah No, it stayed only white, but white is a very good light to see at the end of a long black tunnel you thought would be never ending, that only God or Death could put a stop to, especially when you . . . since I was . . . far from sure about God.

Shannon You're still unsure about him?

Hannah Not as unsure as I was.] You see, in my profession I have to look hard and close at human faces in order to catch something in them before they get restless and call out, 'Waiter, the cheque, we're leaving'. Of course sometimes, a few times, I just see blobs of wet dough that pass for human faces, with bits of jelly for eyes. Then I cue in Nonno to give a recitation, because I can't draw such faces. But those aren't the usual faces, I don't think they're even real. Most time I *do* see something, and I can catch it – I *can*, like I caught something in your face when I sketched you this afternoon with your eyes open. Are you still listening to me? (*He crouches beside her chair, looking up at her intently*.) In Shanghai, Shannon, there is a place that's called the House for the Dying – the old and penniless dying, whose younger, penniless living children and grandchildren take them there for them to get through with their dying on pallets, on straw mats. The first time I went there it shocked me, I ran away from it. But I came back later and I saw that their children and grandchildren and the custodians of the place had put little comforts beside their death-pallets, little flowers and opium candies and religious emblems. That made me able to stay to draw their dying faces. Sometimes only their eyes were still alive, but, Mr Shannon, those eyes of the penniless dying with those last little comforts beside them, I tell you, Mr Shannon, those eyes looked up with their last dim life left in them as clear as the stars in the Southern Cross, Mr Shannon. And now . . . now I am going to say something to you that will sound like something that only the spinster granddaughter of a minor romantic poet is likely to say. . . . Nothing I've ever seen has seemed as beautiful to me, not even the view from this verandah between the sky and the still-water beach, and lately . . . lately my grandfather's eyes have looked up at me like that. . . . (*She rises abruptly and crosses to the front of the verandah*.) Tell me, what is that sound I keep hearing down there?

Don Juan or The Love of Geometry *by Max Frisch (translated by Michael Bullock)*

This play is Max Frisch's loose, ironic take on the story of Don Juan Tenorio, the character of Spanish legend who supposedly to lived in Seville in the fourteenth century and was notorious for his debauchery. It was first staged in 1953.

It begins with Don Juan at twenty-years-old, before he has embarked on his amorous career. Much to his father's frustration he is still a virgin and seems to prefer geometry to women.

This scene takes place in a brothel. Celestina is a famous procuress who numbers bishops amongst her customers. She is a cynical, hard-nosed, businesswoman with no illusions about love. Her job is to sell sex. Her girls are a commodity. She is at the top of her tree – proud of her status in the community and the service she offers. One of her girls, Miranda, has fallen helplessly in love with Don Juan during a visit to the brothel, even though they did nothing but play chess.

Celestina is furious. Falling in love is a cardinal sin for a whore. It is simply not done and Celestina is giving the weeping girl her marching orders. Her ears are closed to Miranda's pleas. A harlot doesn't sell her soul. She has been like a mother to her and this is all the thanks she gets! She berates her for being ungrateful and not taking wise advice. She has heard it all before and has neither patience nor sympathy for Miranda's pathetic snivelling. As far as she's concerned, all men are the same. She knows the game and her clientele inside out and won't have one of her girls behaving 'improperly'. Love is a false emotion and talk of such 'sentimental rubbish' is bad for business.

Celestina In love! And you dare to show your face before me? In love with one man. Here's your bundle and that's the end of it! . . . Didn't I warn you all, over and over again; leave your soul out of it? I know all that nonsense about true love. How else do you think I come to be running a brothel? I know the sob-stuff that starts when the soul comes into it. Once and never again I swore to myself. Haven't I been like a mother to you all? Good God, fancy a beautiful, mercenary creature like you starting to whimper like an animal and babble like a young lady. His hands! His nose! His forehead! And what else has your one and only got? Go on, tell me. His toes! The lobes of his ears! His calves! Go on, what else has he got that's different from everyone else's? But I could see it coming, those downcast eyes the last few weeks – that sentimentality!

[*Miranda* Oh, Celestina, he's not like all the others.

Celestina Get out!

Miranda Oh, Celestina –]

Celestina Get out, I say. For the last time. I won't have sentimental trash on my doorstep. In love with a personality! That's the last straw. And you dare to tell me that to my face, me, Spain's leading procuress. So you're in love with a personality?

[*Miranda* Yes. So help me God.

Celestina speechless.

Miranda Yes.

Celestina That's how you thank me for your education.

Miranda Oh, Celestina –

Celestina Oh, Celestina, oh, Celestina!*] You think you can make fun of me, in the middle of the night, do you? You think you can lie to me like a man? God help you, yes, He'd better – because I certainly shan't, as sure as my name's Celestina. I know what I owe my name. Why do you think the gentlemen come to us? So that you can fall in love, so that you can make distinctions between one and the other?

I keep telling you, day after day: there are girls outside too, women of every age and every degree of willingness, married, unmarried, whatever they like. So why do they come here? I'll tell you, sweetie: here, sweetie, the man recovers from his false emotions. That's what they pay for with silver and gold. What did Don Octavio, the wise judge, say when they wanted to close my house? Leave the good bawd alone, he said, and in public. So long as we have a literature that propagates so many false emotions, we can't do without her – we can't do without her, he said; and that means I am protected by the state. Do you think I should be protected by the state if I allowed anything improper to go on? I don't sell sentiment here. Do you understand? I don't sell girls who inside themselves keep dreaming of another man. Our customers have got plenty of that at home, sweetie; that's not what they come here for! Take your bundle, I say, and get out.

The Open Couple
by Dario Fo and Franca Rame
(translated by Stuart Hood)

The Open Couple was first performed in Italy the early 1980s.
It is a one-act social satire, exploring gender politics through
a middle-class marriage in crisis. The characters are called
Man and Woman. They are stereotypes as much as indivi-
duals, reflecting the role of women in marriage and societies
in which men shape the dominant ideologies.

The couple are in their forties. Man's frequent infidelities
have led to several desperate suicide attempts by Woman.
To revive their relationship the pair agree to give each other
complete sexual freedom. This gives Man permission to
continue his adulterous way of life, but Woman finds it
hard to stray or deal with the emotional backlash of their
open relationship.

At first, Man has the upper hand, indulging in serial
peccadilloes, and expecting his wife to support and
condone them. It is only when Woman falls in love with an
attractive alternative that the tables are turned and Man
begins to reap the painful fruits of his lifestyle choice.

Man and Woman are aware that they are playing
characters in a piece of theatre, and they self-consciously
tell the audience their story. They slip seamlessly back and
forth between scenes from their relationship, to directly
addressing the audience; both commenting on and seeking
support for their various points of view.

At this point Man has asked Woman to take his
schoolgirl mistress to the gynaecologist to fix her up with
some birth control. It's an outrageous request and Woman
shares her anger and incredulity with the audience as she
might with a friend over coffee. She has done her best to
respond to their modern, open relationship in a civilised
way, but this is the last straw. She deals with her feelings by
satirising her role in the affair and making a joke of her
violent response. The tone is cutting, the imagery, amusing
and picturesque. The insult of her husband's affair with a
much younger woman is neatly expressed by references to

playing 'mummy' and 'nanny' to his 'baby dolls'. This is an older woman who has been traded in for a younger model. Angry and jealous, she uses satire and sarcasm as tools to diffuse anger and make light of pain. She paints her husband as an obsessive collector of women, and by using sexist language borrowed from the male vocabulary, she demeans and dismisses them. Her husband's conquests are reduced to impersonal references to the size and shape of their genitalia – metaphors for the way in which his infidelities have invaded every corner of her domestic life.

The couple's attempts to deal with the consequences of their decision are what drive the piece towards its startling and tragic ending.

Woman (*to the audience*) One day my husband comes to me all embarrassed and says:

[*Man*] Listen, this is women's stuff – why don't you go with Paula –

Woman That was the ice-cream girl.

[*Man*] To the gynaecologist and get her fitted with a coil. Maybe you can convince her – she'll go with you – that's for sure.

Woman Yes, of course I'll be mummy little Paula – of course I'll take her to the gynaecologist. 'Doctor, please fit my husband's girl-friend with a coil.' Let's hope he's got as good a sense of humour as we have. I'll fit you with a coil. In your foreskin!

[*Man* (to the audience) *You see how she reacted. And that's nothing.* (To his wife.) *Go on – tell them what you did!*

Woman Yes, I admit I did react.] I'd just finished opening a tin of peeled tomatoes – a 5 kilo one. I poured it over his head and pushed the tin down till it came to his chin – like that. He looked like Sir Lancelot ready for the tournament – sponsored by Buitoni. Then I took advantage of his momentary embarrassment and pushed his hand into the toaster. (*She laughs.*) It was on.

108

[*Man* *Look – I've still got the marks. I looked like a toasted sandwich. I walked about with lettuce leaves between my fingers so that people wouldn't notice.* (To the audience.) *Then the shouts, the insults – a fine open couple – a democratic one.*

Woman *Well, what did you expect?*] I had taken huge steps towards centrifugal sexual freedom – but what a nerve! to want me to play nanny to his baby dolls. I don't know what came over him. He didn't use to be like that. A man possessed. He leapt from one woman to another at the speed of light. I've talked to other women, friends of mine – I did a bit of research. Their husbands are always randy too. It must be a virus – the randicoccus. Even our porter's wife – he's randy – always looking for it. But the fact is that my husband doesn't only look for it, he finds it. He's got a mania. Like those people who look for mushrooms – only one thing on their minds – always going to the woods and collecting masses of them. And then they pickle them! Or dry them. Only he collects – birds, chicks, pussies. I swear – it's got to be an obsession with me. I've gone mad. I kept seeing the house full of female sex organs – used and thrown away! I go into the bathroom and instead of a cake of soap – 'It's a pussy!' I put on my shoes. 'Help – there's a mouse!' No, it's a pussy. There are young ones, intelligent ones, fat ones. How do I keep them alive? I water them. I get the right stuff to keep them alive from the sperm bank where my husband is an honorary member.

The American Dream *by Edward Albee*

This one-act, absurdist comedy premiered in New York in 1961. In Albee's words it is an 'examination of the American Scene, an attack on the substitution of artificial for real values in our society, a condemnation of complacency, cruelty, emasculation and vacuity.'

Mommy and Daddy are an archetypal middle-aged, middle-class couple who have bullied and tortured their adopted son to death because he didn't live up to expectations. Believing they have received a 'faulty' son from the Adoption Agency they demand a refund. When a replacement son arrives, a 'clean-cut, mid-west farm boy type, almost insultingly good looking in a typically American way', Mommy and Daddy get what they think they want. But the Young Man is nearly inhuman in his perfection and dead inside; empty as the American Dream of the title.

This speech comes at the beginning of the play. As Mommy and Daddy wait for someone to come and fix the plumbing, they complain about poor service from underlings, 'people who think they can get away with anything these days'. Mommy provides an example by launching into a seamless diatribe about her attempt to buy a hat. Daddy is indifferent to the story and irritated by Mommy who insists on his attention as she gives him a blow-by-blow account. The tale is boring and inconsequential, but reveals much about Mommy's shallow, self-obsessed nature. She's horrid and patronising to Daddy who has been reduced to nodding agreement. Mommy wears the trousers. Her arbitrary judgements of the chairman (sic) of her woman's club, whom she despises but must be nice to, reveal her as a social-climbing snob. Look how the women call each other 'my dear' – a veneer of good manners for their mutual antipathy. The right coloured hat is clearly a symbol of social standing.

What does the scene in the shop tell us? Mommy must be listened to. Mommy must have satisfaction and she's prepared to do what it takes to get it.

The story is told almost entirely through exchanges of

dialogue. How far you play the other characters is a matter for you to decide, but they certainly should be coloured by Mommy's attitudes to them and her desire to assert her status.

Mommy (*giggles at the thought; then*) All right, now. I went to buy a new hat yesterday and I said, 'I'd like a new hat, please.' And so, they showed me a few hats, green ones and blue ones, and I didn't like any of them, not one bit. What did I say? What did I just say?

[**Daddy** *You didn't like any of them, not one bit.*]

Mommy That's right; you just keep paying attention. And then they showed me one that I did like. It was a lovely little hat, and I said, 'Oh, this is a lovely little hat; I'll take this hat; oh my, it's lovely. What colour is it?' And they said, 'Why, this is beige; isn't it a lovely little beige hat?' And I said, 'Oh, it's just lovely.' And so, I bought it. (*Stops, looks at* **Daddy**.)

[**Daddy** (to show he is paying attention) *And so you bought it.*]

Mommy And so I bought it, and I walked out of the store with the hat right on my head, and I ran spang into the chairman of our woman's club, and she said, 'Oh, my dear, isn't that a lovely little hat? Where did you get that lovely little hat? It's the loveliest little hat; I've always wanted a wheat-coloured hat *myself*.' And I said, 'Why, no, my dear; this hat is beige; beige.' And she laughed and said, 'Why no, my dear, that's a wheat-coloured hat . . . wheat. I know beige from wheat.' And I said, 'Well, my dear, I know beige from wheat, too.' [*What did I say? What did I just say?*

Daddy (tonelessly) *Well, my dear, I know beige from wheat, too.*

Mommy That's right.] And she laughed, and she said, 'Well, my dear, they certainly put one over on you. That's wheat if I ever saw wheat. But it's lovely, just the same.' And then she walked off. She's a dreadful woman, you don't know her; she has dreadful taste, two dreadful children, a dreadful house, and an absolutely adorable

112

husband who sits in a wheel chair all the time. You don't know him. You don't know anybody, do you? She's just a dreadful woman, but she *is* chairman of our woman's club, so naturally I'm terrible fond of her. So, I went right back into the hat shop, and I said, 'Look here; what do you mean selling me a hat that you say is beige, when it's wheat all the time . . . wheat! I can tell beige from wheat any day in the week, but not in this artificial light of yours.' They have artificial light, Daddy.

[*Daddy* Have they!]

Mommy And I said, 'The minute I got outside I could tell that it wasn't a beige hat at all; it was a wheat hat.' And they said to me, 'How could you tell that when you had the hat on the top of your head?' Well, that made me angry, and so I made a scene right there; I screamed as hard as I could; I took my hat off and I threw it down on the counter, and oh, I made a terrible scene. I said, I made a terrible scene.

[*Daddy* (snapping to) *Yes . . . yes . . . good for you!*]

Mommy And I made an absolutely terrible scene; and they became frightened, and they said, 'Oh, madam; oh, madam.' But I kept right on, and finally they admitted that they might have made a mistake; so they took my hat into the back, and then they came out again with a hat that looked exactly like it. I took one look at it, and I said, 'This hat is wheat-coloured; wheat.' Well, of course, they said, 'Oh, no, madam, this hat is beige; you go outside and see.' So, I went outside, and lo and behold, it *was* beige. So I bought it.

Rosalind *by J. M. Barrie*

This poignant little one-act play premiered at the Duke of York's Theatre in 1912. It is about a well-known actress of forty-plus who is tired of 'being 29' all the time. She escapes to a seaside resort where she takes time out to indulge in the 'sloppy, pull-the curtains, carpet slipper' tea drinking comforts of middle-age; but when Charles, a youthful suitor from her other life, turns up on the doorstep the situation becomes rather complicated. A photograph of her alter ego on the mantelpiece, dressed as Shakespeare's Rosalind, exactly matches the one Charles wears next to his heart, leading him to believe that the kindly middle-aged lady in front of him is his beloved's mother. As they talk, however, it emerges to Charles' dismay that they are one and the same person. She feels she owes the poor boy an explanation as to how these painful circumstances came about.

Mrs Beatrice Page is an actress through and through, a 'slave to her public' and with 'a wardrobe' of feelings for every occasion. She is gallant, well-preserved and good-natured. Although here she looks 'an indolent, sloppy thing', dressed in a dowdy dressing gown and large flat slippers, she can nevertheless be theatrical and bewitching with her beautifully modulated voice. With rare insight she freely admits that even when she is crying she is 'looking at you through the corner of her eye to see if she is doing well'. She has invented 'mamma' in order to give her working self a holiday and so she can find out what being middle-aged feels like. But even as she explains, she can't help performing, playing coquettishly on the besotted Charles' feelings, and is by turns delightfully confidential, gleeful and dramatic. We can't help feeling that the middle-aged Mrs Page is just another character in her repertoire. We will never know which is the real Mrs Page: middle-aged 'Mrs Cosy Comfort', or the famous 'twenty-nine-year-old' actress Beatrice. And it seems that neither will she! But as she says, 'Everything is real except middle-age.'

I commend you to Barrie's stage directions which illuminate her character in a most entertaining way.

Mrs Page You have seen lots of plays, Charles?

[*Charles Yes, tons.*]

Mrs Page Have you noticed that there are no parts in them for middle-aged ladies?

[*Charles* (who has had too happy a life to notice this or almost anything else) *Aren't there?*

Mrs Page Oh no, not for 'stars'.] There is nothing for them between the ages of twenty-nine and sixty. Occasionally one of the less experienced dramatists may write such a part, but with a little coaxing we can always make him say, 'She needn't be more than twenty-nine.' And so, dear Charles, we have succeeded in keeping middle-aged women off the stage. Why, even Father Time doesn't let on about us. He waits at the wings with a dark cloth for us, just as our dressers wait with dust-sheets to fling over our expensive frocks; but we have a way with us that makes even Father Time reluctant to cast his cloak; perhaps it is the coquettish imploring look we give him as we dodge him; perhaps though he is an old fellow he can't resist the powder on our pretty noses. And so he says, 'The enchanting baggage, I'll give her another year.' When you come to write my epitaph, Charles, let it be in these delicious words, 'She had a long twenty-nine.'

[*Charles But off the stage – I knew you off.* (Recalling a gay phantom.) *Why, I was one of those who saw you into your train for Monte Carlo.*

Mrs Page You thought you did. That made it easier for me to deceive you here. But I got out of that train at the next station.

She makes a movement to get out of the train here. We begin to note how she suits the action to the word in obedience to Shakespeare's lamentable injunction; she cannot mention the tongs without forking two of her fingers.

Charles You came here instead?

Mrs Page Yes, stole here.

Charles (surveying the broken pieces of her) *Even now I can scarcely— You who seemed so young and gay.Mrs Page* (who is really very good-natured, else would she clout him on the head) *I was a twenty-nine. Oh, don't look so solemn, Charles. It is not confined to the stage. The stalls are full of twenty-nines. Do you remember what fun it was to help me on with my cloak? Remember why I had to put more powder on my chin one evening?*

Charles (with a groan) *It was only a few weeks ago.*

Mrs Page *Yes. Sometimes it was Mr. Time I saw in the mirror, but the wretch only winked at me and went his way.*

Charles (ungallantly) *But your whole appearance – so girlish compared to—*

Mrs Page (gallantly). *To this. I am coming to 'this', Charles.* (Confidentially; no one can be quite so delightfully confidential as **Beatrice Page**.)] You see, never having been more than twenty-nine, not even in my sleep – for we have to keep it up even in our sleep – I began to wonder what middle-age was like. I wanted to feel the sensation. A woman's curiosity, Charles.

[*Charles Still, you couldn't—*

Mrs Page *Couldn't I!*] Listen. Two summers ago, instead of going to Biarritz – see pictures of me in the illustrated papers stepping into my motor-car, or going a round of country houses – see photographs of us all on the steps – the names, Charles, read from left to right – instead of doing any of these things I pretended I went there, and in reality I came down here, determined for a whole calendar month to be a middle-aged lady. I had to get some new clothes, real, cosy, sloppy, very middle-aged clothes; and that is why I invented mamma; I got them for her, you see. I said she was about my figure, but stouter and shorter, as you see she is.

[*Charles* (his eyes wandering up and down her – and nowhere a familiar place) *I can't make out—*

Mrs Page *No, you are too nice a boy to make it out.*] You don't understand the difference that a sober way of doing one's hair, and the letting out of a few strings, and sundry other trifles that are no trifles, make; but you see I vowed that if the immortal part of me was to get a novel sort of rest, my figure should get it also. *Voilà!* And thus all cosy within and without, I took lodgings in the most out-of-the-world spot I knew of, in the hope that here I might find the lady of whom I was in search.

[*Charles Meaning?*]

Mrs Page (*rather grimly*) Meaning myself. Until two years ago she and I had never met.

Equus *by Peter Shaffer*

This is a disturbing play that deals with issues of parenting, religious fervour and our perceptions of normality.

Dora Strang is a former teacher in her forties. She is mother of Alan Strang, a seventeen-year-old boy who has been found guilty of blinding six horses with a metal spike and is undergoing psychiatric treatment. Dora is a conservative, fanatically religious woman who has an almost oedipal connection with her son. She also has a tense relationship with Alan's father, Frank, who bans television, seeks to undermine Dora's religious influence and places a dead hand on everything that makes Alan happy. Both, in their different ways, have cut Alan off from normal life. Alan's relationship with his father is poor so Dora she has been the dominant influence in his life, subjecting him to nightly Bible readings and an abstract, religious interpretation of the meaning of sex.

Dora has just visited Alan at the psychiatric unit. Alan has reacted angrily, throwing his dinner tray at her and staring malevolently, which Dora interprets as blame. Alan's psychiatrist, Martin Dysart, has been called and orders Dora from the room. Both she and Dysart are very upset. In this scene they confront each other. Dysart expresses concern that Dora's visit has disrupted Alan at a delicate stage of his treatment. Dora feels that as a parent she is being blamed for Alan's crime both by Alan and the psychiatric community, and that her distress and needs are being ignored.

Here she is angrily defending herself against all these unspoken accusations – accusations she is projecting onto Dysart. What if her parenting was in some way responsible for the terrible thing Alan has done? In the process of distancing herself from it, she reveals the doubt and guilt she feels. Was it because Frank wouldn't let him watch television? Was it because of the rows? Was it because Frank was too hard on him? She puts words into Dysart's mouth, because these are the questions that keep her awake at night. She can't make any sense of what Alan has done but needs to reject the Freudian explanations, that lay the blame at her door.

Dora is in terrible emotional pain, torn between her love

for her son and the horror and disgust at what he has done. Her explanation that he is 'possessed' by the Devil offers an explanation she can understand and distances both of them from the horrible act.

Dora (*ignoring him: more and more urgently*) Look, Doctor: you don't have to live with this. Alan is one patient to you: one out of many. He's my son. I lie awake every night thinking about it. Frank lies there beside me. I can hear him. Neither of us sleeps all night. You come to us and say, who forbids television? who does what behind whose back? – as if we're criminals. Let me tell you something. We're not criminals. We've done nothing wrong. We loved Alan. We gave him the best love we could. All right, we quarrel sometimes – all parents quarrel – we always make it up. My husband is a good man. He's an upright man, religion or no religion. He cares for his home, for the world, and for his boy. Alan had love and care and treats, and as much fun as any boy in the world. I know about loveless homes: I was a teacher. Our home wasn't loveless. I know about privacy too – not invading a child's privacy. All right, Frank may be at fault here – he digs into him too much – but nothing in excess. He's not a bully . . . (*Gravely.*) No, doctor. Whatever's happened has happened *because of Alan.* Alan is himself. Every soul is itself. If you added up everything we ever did to him, from his first day on earth to this, you wouldn't find why he did this terrible thing – because that's *him*; not just all of our things added up. Do you understand what I'm saying? I want you to understand, because I lie awake and awake thinking it out, and I want you to know that I deny it absolutely what he's doing now, staring at me, attacking me for what *he's* done, for what *he* is! (*Pause, calmer.*) You've got your words, and I've got mine. You call it a complex, I suppose. But if you knew God, Doctor, you would know about the devil. You'd know the Devil isn't made by what mummy says and daddy says. The Devil's *there.* It's an old-fashioned word, but a true thing . . . I'll go. What I did in there was inexcusable. I only know he was my little Alan, and then the Devil came.

A Woman of No Importance
by Oscar Wilde

A Woman of No Importance was first staged in 1893. It shares
themes common to several of Wilde's plays: secret pasts,
fallen women, social criticism and concealed identities.
Although it bristles with Wildean wit and quotable epigrams,
the serious issues of illegitimacy, class and the double
standards of Victorian society are at its heart.

Rachel Arbuthnot is not one of Wilde's witty characters.
She is a handsome woman in her forties with a guilty secret.
Twenty years previously she had an illegitimate child,
Gerald. By re-inventing herself as Mrs Arbuthnot, and
involving herself in the church and 'good works', she has
found a way back into 'society' where she and her son have
been accepted.

Gerald is a personable, sensitive young man, a credit to
his mother, and desperate for advancement. When Gerald
is offered a job as private secretary to the villainous Lord
Illingworth, everyone says he has a brilliant future. It is only
when his mother comes to meet Gerald's 'mentor' that she
finds herself face to face with her past. Lord Illingworth – or
George Harford in an earlier incarnation – is Gerald's father,
the man who seduced his mother, refused to marry her and
abandoned her and her child. If her love for Gerald is the
driving force of her life, it is matched in intensity only by
her loathing for the man she feels ruined it. But Gerald
knows none of this. He is desperate to begin his new career
and cannot understand his mother's objections.

When Gerald discovers the truth, he writes to Lord
Illingworth demanding that he marry his mother and repair
the damage he has caused. In this scene between mother
and son, Gerald tells Mrs Arbuthnot what he has done. She
is horrified. Gerald implores her to set her life to rights by
agreeing to the marriage. He can't understand why any
mother should refuse to marry the father of her child. In
this impassioned speech Mrs Arbuthnot tries to explain her
reasons. The silence is broken. Mrs Arbuthnot masochisti-
cally embraces her sin. It is this and an almost unhealthy
love for her son that defines her. Gerald is the one person in

her life who loves her and to whom she has given uncondi-
tional love. While there can be no doubt of her devotion
and the nobility of her sacrifice, there is also an unexpressed
subtext of possessiveness, emotional blackmail and recrimi-
nation. Strong meat for a sensitive young man! Remember
that Gerald recently made a bid for freedom and she almost
lost him to Lord Illingworth.

The speech pulls out all the emotional stops so you will
need to handle it carefully and truthfully if it is not to sound
melodramatic.

Mrs Arbuthnot Men don't understand what mothers are. I am no
different from other women except in the wrong done me and the
wrong I did, and my very heavy punishments and great disgrace.
And yet, to bear you I had to look on death. To nurture you I had to
wrestle with it. Death fought with me for you. All women have to
fight with death to keep their children. Death, being childless,
wants our children from us. Gerald, when you were naked I clothed
you, when you were hungry I gave you food. Night and day all that
long winter I tended you. No office is too mean, no care too lowly
for the thing we women love – and oh! how *I* loved *you*. Not
Hannah, Samuel more. And you needed love, for you were weakly,
and only love could have kept you alive. Only love can keep anyone
alive. And boys are careless often and without thinking give pain,
and we always fancy that when they come to man's estate and
know us better they will repay us. But it is not so. The world draws
them from our side, and they make friends with whom they are
happier than they are with us, and have amusements from which
we are barred, and interests that are not ours: and they are unjust to
us often, for when they find life bitter they blame us for it, and
when they find it sweet we do not taste its sweetness with them. . . .
You made many friends and went into their houses and were glad
with them, and I, knowing my secret, did not dare to follow, but
stayed at home and closed the door, shut out the sun and sat in
darkness. What should I have done in honest households? My past

was ever with me. . . . And you thought I didn't care for the pleasant things of life. I tell you I longed for them, but did not dare to touch them, feeling I had no right. You thought I was happier working amongst the poor. That was my mission, you imagined. It was not, but where else was I to go? The sick do not ask if the hand that smoothes their pillow is pure, nor the dying care if the lips that touch their brow have known the kiss of sin. It was you I thought of all the time; I gave to them the love you did not need: lavished on them a love that was not theirs. . . . And you thought I spent too much of my time in going to Church, and in Church duties. But where else could I turn? God's house is the only house where sinners are made welcome, and you were always in my heart, Gerald, too much in my heart. For, though day after day, at morn or evensong, I have knelt in God's house, I have never repented of my sin. How could I repent of my sin when you, my love, were its fruit! Even now that you are bitter to me I cannot repent. I do not. You are more to me than innocence. I would rather be your mother – oh! much rather! – than have been always pure. . . . Oh, don't you see? don't you understand? It's my dishonour that has made you so dear to me. It is my disgrace that has bound you so closely to me. It is the price I paid for you – the price of soul and body – that makes me love you as I do. Oh, don't ask me to do this horrible thing. Child of my shame, be still the child of my shame!

Dona Rosita the Spinster
by Frederico Garcia Lorca
(translated by Gwynn Edwards)

This play received a triumphant premiere in Barcelona in 1935. Lorca's inspiration was a seventeenth-century story about a 'mutable rose' and the play is a metaphor for the passing of time, disillusion and the fading of hopes and dreams. Each of the three acts symbolise a stage in a journey from early love to abandonment and desolation. It is set in Granada between 1855 and 1911.

The central character is Rosita, a pretty, young woman in love with her cousin. She is an orphan who has been brought up by a loving aunt and an uncle who is passionate about his flowers, but who has no head for business. When Rosita's lover is called away to look after his ageing parents' farm, he promises to return and marry her. Years pass and Rosita waits faithfully, sustained by his love letters, but her fiancé betrays her and marries someone else. Rosita tries to deny the truth and hang onto her dream, but local title-tattle and pitying looks force her to confront the truth about her wasted life.

In the final act Rosita is forty-five. Her uncle has died. He had raised a mortgage against the family home to pay for Rosita's furniture and trousseaux. Now the house is being sold from under them, leaving only the barest necessities. Rosita's aunt, who out of love has continued to feed Rosita's hopes of marriage, is almost destitute. Rosita waits with her aunt while the removal men empty the house.

Rosita is in a state of emotional emptiness. She is describing a lifetime of denial – giving voice to the loneliness and humiliation that have dogged her life. The repeated phrases and insistent rhythms hammer out the passage of time; the long arching sentences articulate the intensity of the emotion that underpins them. The loss of the house brings the truth into the open and Rosita finally accepts her life as a lost cause.

Rosita (*kneeling*) I've become accustomed to living outside myself for many years now, thinking about things that were far away . . . And now that these things no longer exist, I find myself going around and around in a cold place, searching for a way out that I'll never find . . . I knew the truth. I knew he'd got married. A kind soul insisted on telling me, but I went on receiving his letters with an illusion full of sadness that surprised even me . . . If no one had said anything; if you hadn't known; if only I had known the truth, his letters and his deceit would have fed my dream as they did in the first year of his absence. But everyone knew the truth and I'd find myself picked out by a pointing finger that ridiculed the modesty of a girl soon to be married and made grotesque the fan of a girl who was still single. Each year that passed was like an intimate piece of clothing torn from my body. One day a friend gets married, and then another, and yet another, and the next day she has a son, and the son grows up and comes to show me his examination marks. Or there are new houses and new songs. And there am I, with the same trembling excitement, cutting the same carnations, looking at the same clouds. And then one day I'm out walking, and I suddenly realise I don't know anyone. Girls and boys leave me behind because I can't keep up, and one of them says: 'There's the old maid'; and another one, a good-looking boy with curly hair says: 'No one's going to fancy her again.' I hear it all and I can't protest against it. I can only go on, with a mouth full of bitterness and a great desire to run away, to take off my shoes, to rest and never move again from my corner.

[**Aunt** *Oh, Rosita, my child!*

Rosita I'm too old now.] Yesterday I heard the housekeeper say that I'd still be able to marry. Never! Don't even think it! I lost that hope when I lost the man I wanted with all my blood, the man I loved . . . and go on loving. Everything's finished . . . and yet, with all my dreams destroyed, I go to bed and get up again with the terrible feeling that hope is finally dead . . . I want to run away, not to be able to see, to be calm, empty . . . Doesn't a poor woman have the right to breathe freely? And yet hope pursues me, circles around me, gnaws at me: like a dying wolf trying to sink his teeth in for the last time.

Filulmena Marturano *by Eduardo de Filippo (translated by Carlo Ardito)*

De Fillipo's boisterous and touching play *Filumena Marturano* is set in post-Second World War Naples and presents us with a vibrant slice of Neopolitan family life. It is the story of Shakespeare's *Taming of the Shrew* in reverse, as in this case it is a wife who brings a recalcitrant husband to heel. It was first staged in 1946 and is one of de Filippo's most successful plays.

Filumena is a strong, kind, proud and loving Italian, the uncomplaining housekeeper and mistress to wealthy businessman Domenico Soriano. Since Domenico took her from a brothel to share his life, she has received little appreciation or affection over twenty five years of service. She is described in the stage directions as 'a youthful forty-eight. Traces of her working-class background show and she makes no attempt to conceal them. Her manner is open, her voice always frank and decisive. She is the sort of woman who prefers to face up to life in her own independent way.'

When Domenico announces his intention to marry a nubile and sprightly younger woman instead of her, Filumena takes to her bed and tricks Domenico into a deathbed marriage. The play begins at the point when the newly wed makes an unexpected recovery. Domenico is furious at being duped, but there is more to come. Filumena reveals that she has three grown-up sons, fathered by former 'clients', living close by. None of them know who she is. She adds insult to injury by telling Domenico that she has anonymously provided for them with money she has stolen from him over the years. She tells him she wants her sons to be legitimised by taking his name. One of them is Domenico's, though she won't say which for fear of him receiving preferential treatment.

In this scene all three sons have been summoned to the house and Filumena announces publicly that she is their mother. It is a bit of a bombshell. In this candid and confessional speech she tells them about her squalid family background and how she was driven by poverty, and tempted by material things, into the brothel where Domenico found her. This is the lioness, who did what she had to do to survive and protect her young. Now she needs to explain. She has always loved her man and her children. Her end game is for them all, finally, to be a family after so much wasted time.

[**Domenico** (accommodatingly) *Please don't* . . .]

Filumena Be quiet! (**Riccardo, Umberto** *and* **Michele** *come in from the terrace.* **Rosalia** *enters upstage right at the same time carrying a tray with three cups of coffee, but sensing the awkwardness of the situation puts down the tray and settles down to listen. Addresses* **Riccardo, Umberto** *and* **Michele**.) These gentlemen are men of the world. The world with all its laws and rights, the sort of world that fends off trouble and inconvenience with scraps of paper. (*Points to herself.*) Here on the other hand am I: Filumena Marturano, the freak that can't even cry. Dummi': isn't this what people have been saying about me? – 'Have you ever seen a tear in her eyes?' Well, I'm running true to form, and without so much as a sob – you can see my eyes are as dry as dust – (*Stares at the three young men.*) I am your mother!

[**Domenico** *Filume'* . . .]

Filumena (*firmly*) Who are you to stop me saying, in front of my sons, that I am their mother? (*To* **Nocella**.) Is there a law to prevent it? (*Aggressively.*) Yes, you are my sons. And I am Filumena Marturano – need I say more? You are grown men and I suppose you've heard people talk about me. (*The three stand as if petrified.* **Umberto** *has gone pale.* **Riccardo** *looks at his shoes in embarrassment,* **Michele** *looks astonished and moved.*) I became what I became when I was seventeen. (*Pause.*) Mr Nocella, do you know about slums? The ones at San Giovanni, at Vergini, at Forcella, Tribunale or Pallunnetto? Black, smoky hovels . . . there's so many people to a room that in summer it's so hot you can't stand it, and so cold in winter that your teeth chatter. That's where I come from, from one such slum in the Vico San Liborio. As for my family there were so

128

many of us I lost count. I don't know what's happened to them and frankly I'm not interested. All I can recall are sad, hungry faces, always at odds with each other. You would go to sleep at night and nobody ever said goodnight. We'd wake up the following day and no one ever said good morning. The only 'kind' word that was ever said to me came from my father . . . and I still shudder at the memory of it. I was thirteen at the time. He said: You're getting to be a big girl, and there isn't much to eat in this house, you know . . . And the heat. At night, with the door shut, you couldn't breathe. We'd sit around the table . . . there was just one big dish and heaven knows how many forks. I may have imagined it, but I felt that every time I dipped my fork into the dish they were looking at me disapprovingly, as though I were stealing that food. When I was seventeen I began to notice how well dressed some people were. Young women with pretty shoes walking past . . . I just stared. One evening I came across a girl I knew: she was so well turned out I hardly recognised her. In those days I attached more importance than I do now to that sort of thing. She said to me: (*Articulates the words with care.*) You just do this . . . this . . . and this . . . I couldn't sleep all night. God, and that heat. (*To* **Domenico**.) That's when we met. (**Domenico** *gives a start.*) In that 'house' which to my eyes was like a palace at first. My heart beat so fast the evening I went back to the Vico San Liborio! I thought: They'll throw me out, shut the door in my face! But nobody said a word. On the contrary: one gave me a chair, another stroked my cheek . . . they all stared at me as though I was in some way superior to them. They were ill at ease in my presence. It was only my mother . . . when I went up to her to say goodbye, who looked away from me, sobbing. I never went back there again. (*Loud.*) I haven't killed my sons! I've looked after *my* family for twenty-five years! (*To* **Riccardo, Umberto** *and* **Michele**.) I've brought you up, made men out of you. I stole from him so you'd be well looked after!

A Night Out *by Harold Pinter*

A Night Out is a short, dark drama about a young man's efforts to escape from his mother. It was first performed on the BBC Third Programme in 1960.

Mrs Stokes is a widow in her fifties. She lives in a small house in south London with her son, Albert. She is lonely and controlling, keeping twenty-eight-year-old Albert on a short leash. Albert survives by a mixture of compliance, tactful management and silent rebellion. On this particular evening, Albert determines to go out to a works leaving-do in spite of his mother's efforts to stop him. Once there, however, the evening blows up in his face when he is falsely accused of sexually harassing a female colleague, and it deteriorates still further when his friends taunt him for being a 'mummy's boy'. A fight ensues. Angry and disconcerted, Albert stays out late.

His mother waits up for him and catches him trying to sneak past her up the stairs. Worried where he has been and furious he didn't come home when he said he would, she launches into him with this monologue. She attacks on every vulnerable front. Accusation, reproach, mockery and emotional blackmail are all used to devastating effect. She harangues her son on the state of his clothes, his lack of consideration, his loose behaviour and his lack of love, groundlessly speculating about the debauched life he leads outside the house.

One of Pinter's great skills is to convey layers of meaning in even the most banal dialogue, revealing pre-occupations that his characters are at pains to conceal. Mrs Stokes' loneliness, feelings of worthlessness, and a fear that Albert will be seduced away from her by the flesh-pots of the outside world are what underpin this speech. Hers is an obsessive, destructive kind of love that is rooted in her own need and that expresses itself in a destructive will to control Albert's life. Look at the pressure she exerts on him to eat his dinner: shepherds pie means 'love' to Mrs Stokes, 'control' to Albert.

Pay careful attention to the stage directions and the pauses. They are full of the unspoken tensions between mother and son, with Albert's intransigent silences goading his mother on to fresh and more damaging attack. Unknown to Mrs Stokes, the evening's events have disturbed the delicate balance of their relationship and Albert is building up a dangerous head of steam.

Look at the last ten lines. They are punctuated only by commas. Mrs Stokes scarcely draws breath as her critical, blackmailing, controlling vitriol gains savage momentum. Renewed efforts to make Albert eat his dinner finally push him over the edge.

The kitchen.

Mrs Stokes *is asleep, her head resting on the table, the cards disordered. The clock ticks. It is twelve o'clock. The front door opens slowly.* **Albert** *comes in, closes the door softly, stops, looks across to the open kitchen door, sees his mother, and begins to creep up the stairs with great stealth. The camera follows him. Her voice stops him.*

Mother Albert!

He stops.

Albert! Is that you?

She goes to the kitchen door.

What are you creeping up the stairs for? Might have been a burglar. What would I have done then?

He descends slowly.

Creeping up the stairs like that. Give anyone a fright. Creeping up the stairs like that. You leave me in the house all alone . . . (*She stops and regards him.*) Look at you! Look at your suit. What's the matter with your tie, it's all crumpled, I pressed it for you this morning. Well, I won't even ask any questions. That's all. You look a disgrace.

He walks past her into the kitchen, goes to the sink and pours himself a glass of water. She follows him.

What have you been doing, mucking about with girls?

She begins to pile the cards.

Mucking about with girls, I suppose. Do you know what the time is? I fell asleep, right here at this table, waiting for you. I don't know what your father would say. Coming in this time of night. It's after twelve o'clock. In a state like that. Drunk, I suppose. I suppose your dinner's ruined. Well, if you want to make a convenience out of your own home, that's your business. I'm only your mother, I don't suppose that counts for much these days. I'm not saying any more. If you want to go mucking about with girls, that's your business.

She takes his dinner out of the oven.

Well, anyway, you'll have your dinner. You haven't eaten a single thing all night.

She places a plate on the table and gets knife and fork. He stands by the sink, sipping water.

I wouldn't mind if you found a really nice girl and brought her home and introduced her to your mother, brought her home for dinner, I'd know you were sincere, if she was a really nice girl, she'd be like a daughter to me. But you've never brought a girl home here in your life. I suppose you're ashamed of your mother.

Pause.

Come on, it's all dried up. I kept it on a low light. I couldn't even go up to Grandma's room and have a look round because there wasn't any bulb, you might as well eat it.

He stands.

What's the matter, are you drunk? Where did you go, to one of those pubs in the West End? You'll get into serious trouble, my boy, if you frequent those places, I'm warning you. Don't you read the papers?

Pause.

132

I hope you're satisfied, anyway. The house in darkness, I wasn't going to break my neck going down to that cellar to look for a bulb, you come home looking like I don't know what, anyone would think you gave me a fortune out of your wages. Yes. I don't say anything, do I? I keep quiet about what you expect me to manage on. I never grumble. I keep a lovely home, I bet there's none of the boys in your firm better fed than you are. I'm not asking for gratitude. But one thing hurts me, Albert, and I'll tell you what it is. Not for years, not for years, have you come up to me and said, Mum, I love you, like you did when you were a little boy. You've never said it without me having to ask you. Not since before your father died. And he was a good man. He had high hopes of you. I've never told you, Albert, about the high hopes he had of you. I don't know what you do with all your money. But don't forget what it cost us to rear you, my boy, I've never told you about the sacrifices we made, you wouldn't care, anyway. Telling me lies about going to the firm's party. They've got a bit of respect at that firm, that's why we sent you there, to start off your career, they wouldn't let you carry on like that at one of their functions. Mr King would, have his eye on you. I don't know where you've been. Well, if you don't want to lead a clean life it's your lookout, if you want to go mucking about with all sorts of bits of girls, if you're content to leave your own mother sitting here till midnight, and I wasn't feeling well, anyway, I didn't tell you because I didn't want to upset you, I keep things from you, you're the only one I've got, but what do you care, you don't care, you don't care, the least you can do is sit down and eat the dinner I cooked for you, specially for you, it's Shepherd's Pie—

Albert *lunges to the table, picks up the clock and violently raises it above his head. A stifled scream from the* **Mother.**

The Glass Menagerie *by Tennessee Williams*

This loosely autobiographical 'memory' play premiered in 1945 and established Tennessee Williams as a major playwright. It is considered a masterpiece of modern theatre.

The drama centres on the dysfunctional Wingfield family and their struggle for survival during the Great Depression in America in the 1930s. Amanda shares a cramped apartment in downtown St. Louis with her daydreaming son Tom and handicapped daughter Laura. All of them in their different ways long for escape. The children's father abandoned the family years earlier, leaving an unrepentant note before 'skipping the light fantastic out of town'. The family survives on Tom's reluctant employment in a warehouse. Amanda longs for her fragile daughter to have a gentleman caller, to save her from impending spinsterhood.

Amanda is an ageing southern belle, a foolish matriarch – all sugar and spite and shabby gentility. Tennessee Williams describes her as 'a woman of great but confused vitality clinging frantically to another time and place'. She is a complex character with 'as much to love and pity as there is to laugh at. She has endurance and a kind of heroism, and though her foolishness makes her unwittingly cruel at times, there is tenderness in her slight person'.

She foolishly hankers for a lost Mississippi youth of gentlemen callers, and in this speech is regaling her children with stories about them. Her stories transport her back to the time and place when she was a popular Blue Mountain debutante, loved and courted by all the rich, clever and handsome young men of the county. She was the most sought after, the most beautiful. She speaks in an exaggerated Southern drawl, posturing ridiculously as she tells her children of all the missed opportunities of her youth, the excitement of it all, and the love she could not requite. It is an oft-told tale and certainly as much fantasy as reality (seventeen at a time?), but it enables her to escape from her grim circumstances into a poetic rapture of youthful passion and romance. These are fantasies to keep out the dark. It is only when we get to the last line of the speech that we have any inkling of the deep disappointment that lives at the heart of her life.

Amanda Girls in those days *knew* how to talk, I can tell you.

[*Tom* Yes?

Image on screen: **Amanda** as a girl on a porch, greeting callers.]

Amanda They knew how to entertain their gentlemen callers. It wasn't enough for a girl to be possessed of a pretty face and a graceful figure – although I wasn't slighted in either respect. She also needed to have a nimble wit and a tongue to meet all occasions.

[*Tom* What did you talk about?

Amanda Things of importance going on in the world! Never anything coarse or common or vulgar.]

She addresses **Tom** *as though he were seated in the vacant chair at the table though he remains by the portieres. He plays this scene as though reading from a script.*

My callers were gentlemen – all! Among my callers were some of the most prominent young planters of the Mississippi Delta – planters and sons of planters!

Tom *motions for music and a spot of light on* **Amanda**. *Her eyes lift, her face glows, her voice becomes rich and elegiac.*

Screen legend: 'Ou sont les neiges d'antan?'

There was young Champ Laughlin who later became vice-president of the Delta Planters Bank. Hadley Stevenson who was drowned in Moon Lake and left his widow one hundred and fifty thousand in Government bonds. There were the Cutrere brothers, Wesley and Bates. Bates was one of my bright particular beaux! He got in a quarrel with that wild Wainwright boy. They shot it out on the floor of Moon Lake Casino. Bates was shot through the stomach.

Died in the ambulance on his way to Memphis. His widow was also well provided-for, came into eight or ten thousand acres, that's all. She married him on the rebound – never loved her – carried my picture on him the night he died! And there was that boy that every girl in the Delta had set her cap for! That beautiful, brilliant young Fitzhugh boy from Greene County!

[*Tom What did he leave his widow?*

Amanda He never married! Gracious, you talk as though all of my admirers had turned up their toes to the daisies!

Tom Isn't this the first you've mentioned that still survives?]

Amanda That Fitzhugh boy went North and made a fortune – came to be known as the Wolf of Wall Street! He had the Midas touch, whatever he touched turned to gold! And I could have been Mrs Duncan J. Fitzhugh, mind you! But – I picked your *father!*

Absolutely! (perhaps) *by Luigi Pirandello (adapted by Martin Sherman)*

Italian playwright Luigi Pirandello wrote *Absolutely! (perhaps)* in 1917. It was the play that won him international recognition.

The action focuses on a single situation involving the arrival in town of Signora Frola, her daughter and son-in law – refugees from an outlying village that has been devastated by an earthquake. They arouse the speculation of townsfolk when it appears that, although Signora Frola lives nearby and visits her daughter twice a day, she is forbidden from entering her house. She only ever speaks to her from a courtyard, never sees her and exchanges letters via a basket that is pulled to her balcony by a rope. Is her daughter sick? A prisoner? Dead? Is Signora Frola mad? Curiosity and gossip run rife.

Signora Frola is a dignified, elderly, motherly woman who has lost all her relatives in the earthquake except her daughter and son-in-law. She is described as 'a pleasant woman, modest and friendly. Her eyes seem sad, but they are offset by a constant smile.' In this scene she has been quizzed by the townsfolk about her strange domestic arrangements and has managed to field their questions with tact and dignified civility. Her son-in–law, however, refutes her account, claiming the reason for her strange behaviour is that she has gone mad with grief because her daughter is in fact dead and he has married someone else. At this point she feels compelled to tell her own version of events.

She speaks of her son-in-law with great compassion and understanding, arguing it is he who is unhinged. She is a powerful advocate for his behaviour, explaining it as the product of an excess of love and describing how he nearly destroyed her daughter with his overbearing passion. As a result, she and her daughter must humour him in the conceit that he is married a second time in order to maintain the equilibrium of their lives.

It is a strange and persuasive tale, leaving the townsfolk uncertain what to believe. Which story is true? How can they know? What is illusion and what is reality? People are not always as they seem. Is Signora Frola telling the truth? How much difference will that make to the way you deliver this speech? You must decide this when you have read the play.

The play addresses philosophical questions about perception. When the audience and townsfolk are confronted with two versions of the same story they discover that neither presents them with a single verifiable truth.

Signora Frola No! Listen to me, please. He is not mad. You have seen him yourselves; surely you observed his strength; his physical strength – he is very robust. When he married he was caught in a storm, a tornado, a veritable hurricane of love. No, more than love – *desire*. Desire so strong, so physically overbearing it threatened to destroy my daughter, who was rather . . . delicate. I trust you take my meaning. She stopped eating. She had a complete breakdown. The doctors advised a rest cure, as indeed did all our relatives, those who have tragically perished in the earthquake. She was placed into a sanatorium. Well, you can imagine what effect this had on him. His monumental passion had no outlet. He fell into a morbid depression. He was convinced that his wife was dead. He went into mourning. He dressed in black. Nothing could convince him that she was alive, only . . . away. Finally, my daughter recovered. She was beautiful and healthy once again. She returned to his house. He refused to acknowledge her. He looked at her and said, 'No . . . no . . . this is not my wife. My wife is dead.' Then he would look at her again and his eyes seemed to recognise her, but the moment passed, and again he said, 'No . . . no . . . this is not she.' There was only one thing for us to do. We had to pretend that my daughter was indeed another woman. We pretended to have a second wedding. He thinks she is his second wife. And he is gentler with her now. But she is not his second wife. She is his first.

[*Signora Sirelli* That explains why he says –

Signora Frola What he says and what he thinks are possibly quite different.] He may not really believe this charade. Deep in his heart, he may know the truth. But he mustn't say it out loud. He must persuade everyone that she is his second wife. That is the only way he can feel safe. For he is afraid she will be taken away again. (*Smiles.*) And so he keeps her to himself. And for himself. Do you see? He worships her. And my daughter has grown to need his love. She is finally . . . content. (*Rises.*) I must leave. If he finds I'm not at home, he'll work himself up into even more of a state. (*Sighs.*) This deception takes a lot of patience. My daughter must pretend she is someone else and I have to pretend that I am mad. But what choice do we have? As long as he's happy. Please, don't get up. I know the way out. Good afternoon.

She bows and smiles and hurries out.

Pour Lucrece *by Jean Giraudoux* *(translated as* Duel of Angels *by Christopher Fry)*

Duel of Angels is set in Aix-en-Provence in the mid-nineteenth century. Giraudoux uses as his inspiration the legend of the rape of Lucrece, in which a Roman gentlewoman chooses suicide over dishonour. This is a complexly plotted and stylishly written tragedy in which vice and virtue do battle for the soul of womanhood, leaving the audience uncertain as to which does most harm!

Aix-en-Provence had a climate that 'bred love like a fever and nobody minded'. But when the moralistic Justice Blanchard arrives he declares it 'as bad as Sodom and Gomorrah' and metes out rough justice on its citizens.

Under this regime, virtue in the shape of Blanchard's wife, Lucile, confronts vice in the shape of beautiful and adulterous Paola. Paola's husband, Armand, is blissfully ignorant of his wife's infidelities until Lucile takes it upon herself to tell him, thereby destroying his love and peace of mind. Paola not only sees this as a personal betrayal but as a betrayal of womankind; she enlists the aid of Barbette, an elderly brothel-keeper, to devise a suitably just revenge.

Lucile is drugged, put to bed in one Barbette's 'houses' and set up with evidence to suggest she has been raped in her sleep by Count Marcellus, the town's notorious seducer. Ensuing revelations leave Marcellus dead, Lucile distraught and Armand fleeing from justice, while Lucile's self-righteous husband abandons her because she is no long 'pure'. Finding herself surrounded by corruption, Lucile kills herself – claiming a victory for virtue as she dies.

This is the last speech of the play. A contrite Barbette is alone and preparing Lucile's body for burial. Barbette's character only appears briefly before this, but we know she is a wily, unprincipled old whore who can be bought. Paola describes her as 'Barbette the blood-letter', and she has strange powers too. For instance, she offers Paola a variety of options for revenge on Lucile: 'a thorn in a facial nerve', 'a drug to make her come out in sores', to 'cut off her eyelashes', or to 'make her grow a moustache'. She is something of an apothecary then, and, perhaps, something of a sorceress? She talks to the corpse lovingly, like a mother or a confidant. The fact that she was an instrument in Lucile's death escapes her. Even as she extols Lucile's virtues, she steals jewellery from the body.

Barbette's speech is a postscript for the playwright, offering insights and explanations for what has gone before.

———————

Barbette Dear little creature, my little angel! The others have gone, and now we can talk. There's only God between us, and he has been with you since yesterday. If you had seen how you got up from the bed at midnight, you would know. It was a miracle . . . All the women in the town are talking about it already. You crossed yourself, and your stockings drew themselves on by themselves. Your shoes slipped themselves on to your feet. People have been canonized for less. The flowers I'd put at the bedside, my paper flowers, they breathed out the scent of roses, and when I went to touch them the flowers and the leaves were real. I'm not lying, I promise you; and just let me take this little ring off your finger to keep as a memory of it. You're thinner than you were yesterday, my angel: the ring comes off of its own accord. Mind you, miracles don't make our job any easier: they are bad for business. Purity's not for this world, but every ten years we get a gleam of it. And now all of them, with their intrigues and wicked doings, are going to see themselves standing in the light of it. Standing stock still, looking surprised, as though the photographer was taking them, as though the pure light was drenching their bodies. They will suddenly see it for the holy thing it was, and they'll feel it reproach them . . . It won't last long with them, I know that very well. With women the virtue of one is the virtue of all. Whereas each man lives the lord of his own dunghill, and has to be his own saint, and his own purgatory. Get along with you. We've all understood you; Paola as much as anybody. It's true you were ravished. But not by Marcellus. You could have got over that, fifty women have got over that; you knew yourself you could. But what struck you down was being made aware of man's stupidity, and coarseness, and wickedness, too much all of a sudden. And if you're as tender a creature as you, you die of it. Your brooch is coming undone; that means you're giving it to me, and I'm taking it for a keepsake. There's only this mark of the bite my old mouth gave you that you'll have to explain up there, but don't think twice about it. Show it to them, explain. Tell them it's a kiss to all women from an old bawd in Aix, and you've brought it along as a promise from her that she, and all her sisters of the town, won't give men any rest, neither in the profession nor on the side, neither to the young ones who snigger like fools, nor the old ones with their lecherous grinning, nor the handsome ones, nor the ugly ones, nor the city treasurer, nor the magistrate's clerk who comes as a spy: give no rest to their health, nor their purse, nor their family, nor the marrow of their bones, so as to revenge you, my little angel, and lead them all straight to eternal damnation. Amen.

Ubu Rex *by Alfred Jarry*
(translated by Cyril Connolly and Simon Watson Taylor)

Alfred Jarry is primarily known for his *Ubu* plays, which started out as puppet shows devised with teenage friends, to lampoon their physics teacher. They are seen as theatre's first pieces of absurdist drama and have had a profound influence on both the French surrealist movement and the work of such playwrights as Beckett and Inoesco.

Ubu Rex was first performed in France in 1896. It mirrors Shakespeare's *Macbeth* and can be seen as a sideswipe at society's empty values and the indifference of our masters. It was received with a mixture of outrage and controversy by the chattering classes of the day and was the only play of the cycle to be performed in Jarry's short lifetime.

Pa Ubu is a repellent, murderous, old man, who usurps the throne of Poland by every foul means. His wife, Ma Ubu, is an objectionable, greedy slattern. Like Ubu she is a grotesque – a larger than life character who is self-interested, cruel, manipulative and over- indulgent. They embody everything that is base and stupid in the human race. Once the pair achieve power they embark on a brutal and tyrannical rule until they are driven from the land by opposing forces.

This scene comes quite near the end of the play. The Ubus have been dethroned after a terrific battle and forced to flee. Ma Ubu has run off with the state treasures and Palcontent Gyron, a handsome Balonian soldier. After a hair-raising flight from the capital, involving narrowly escaping from death-by-stoning and the horrific demise of her lover, she has found shelter for the night. She speaks directly to the audience, graphically describing all the violent encounters and misfortunes that have befallen her. She is exhausted and hungry, but is safe at last and beginning to relish how she has 'skinned' her objectionable spouse and 'relieved him of his rix-dollars!'

This play pays no lip service to social realism. Jarry's characters are vulgar, shockingly dehumanised and over the top. The language is gross, idiosyncratic and colourful – littered with invented words like *rix-dollars* and *phynance charger*, and childish expletives like *Biff, bam, boom*. The style is energetic and broad brush. Think Punch and Judy; think vaudeville; think pantomime; think Monty Python; think The Goons, and you will begin to have some understanding of Jarry's surreal and exuberant world.

It is night. **Pa Ubu** *is asleep.* **Ma Ubu** *enters without seeing him. It is pitch dark.*

Ma Ubu Shelter at last! I'm alone here, which is fine as far as I'm concerned, but what a dreadful journey: crossing the whole of Poland in four days! Every possible misfortune struck me at the same moment. As soon as that great, fat oaf had clattered off on his nag I crept into the crypt to grab the treasure, but then everything went wrong. I just escaped being stoned to death by Boggerlas and his madmen. I lost my gallant Palcontent Gyron who was so enamoured of my charms that he swooned with delight every time he saw me and even, I've been told, every time he didn't see me – and there can be no higher love than that. Poor boy, he would have let himself be cut in half for my sake, and the proof is that Boggerlas cut him in quarters. Biff, bam, boom! Ooh, I thought it was all up with me. Then I fled for my life with the bloodthirsty mob hard on my heels. I managed to get out of the palace and reach the Vistula, but all the bridges were guarded. I swam across the river, hoping to shake off my pursuers. The entire nobility rallied and joined in the chase. I nearly breathed my last a thousand times, half smothered by the surrounding Poles all screaming for my blood. Finally, I escaped their clutches, and after four days of trudging through the snows of what was once my kingdom have at last reached refuge here. I've had nothing to eat or drink these past four days, and Boggerlas breathing down my neck the whole time. Now here I am, safe at last. Ah! I'm dead with exhaustion and hunger. But I'd give a lot to know what became of my big fat buffoon, I mean to say my esteemed spouse. Lord, how I've skinned him, and relieved him of his rix-dollars! I've certainly rolled him plenty! And his phynance charger that was dying of hunger – it didn't get oats to munch very often, poor beast! It was fun while it lasted, but alas, I had to leave my treasure behind in Warsaw, where it's up for grabs.

Acknowledgements

p.111   extract from *The American Dream* by Edward Albee (published in *New American Drama*, Penguin, 1966). Copyright © Edward Albee. Performance rights: The Dramatists Play Service, Inc., USA, www.dramatists.com.

p.91   extract from *The Rehearsal* by Jean Anouilh, from Anouilh Plays 2, Methuen Drama. Copyright © 1991 Jeremy Sams. Performance rights: Alan Brodie Representation Ltd, www.alanbrodie.com.

p.28   extract from *Confusions* by Alan Ayckbourn, Methuen Drama. Copyright © 1977 by Redburn Productions Ltd. Professional performance rights: Casarotto Ramsay & Associates Ltd, www.casarotto.uk.com. Amateur performance rights: Samuel French Ltd, www.samuelfrench-london.co.uk.

p.114   extract from *Rosalind* by J M Barrie, from *The Plays of J M Barrie*, Hodder & Stoughton, 1929. Published by permission of Samuel French Ltd on behalf of the Estate of J M Barrie. Performance rights: Samuel French Ltd, www.samuelfrench-london.co.uk

p.14   extract from *The Springtime of Others* by Jean-Jacques Bernard. Published in *The Sulky Fire: Five Plays* by Jonathan Cape, 1948. Translation copyright © John Leslie Frith.

p.37   extract from *The Good Person of Setzuan* by Bertolt Brecht, translated by Eric Bentley, Originally published in *Parables of the Theatre*, Penguin, 1965. Translation copyright © Stefan Brecht. Professional performance rights (except US & Canada): Alan Brodie Representation Ltd, www.alanbrodie.com. Amateur performance rights (except US & Canada): Samuel French Ltd, www.samuelfrench-london.co.uk. US & Canadian performance rights: Jerold L Couture, Fitelson, Lasky, Aslan & Couture, 551 Fifth Avenue, New York, NY 10176-0078, USA.

p.46   extract from *Wine in the Wilderness* by Alice Childress. For all rights contact: Douglas & Kopelman Artists, Inc., 393 West 49th Street, 5G, New York, NY 10019, USA.

p.57   extract from *The Unexpected Guest* by Agatha Christie, published by Samuel French London, 1958. Estate representative and performance rights contact: Aitken Alexander Associates Ltd, www.aitkenalexander.co.uk.

p.31   extract from *Early Mourning* (or *Sorry You've Been Troubled*) by

Noël Coward, from *Collected Revue Sketches and Parodies*, Methuen Drama. Copyright © The Estate of Noël Coward. Performance rights: Alan Brodie Representation Ltd, www.alanbrodie.com.

p.127   extract from *Filumena Marturano* by Eduardo de Filippo, from *De Filippo Four Plays*, Methuen Drama. Translation copyright © 1976 Carlo Ardito. Performance rights: Alan Brodie Representation Ltd, www.alanbrodie.com in the first instance.

p.48   extract from *Eden Cinema* by Marguerite Duras, from *Duras Four Plays*, Oberon Books. Copyright © Mercure de France. Translation copyright © Barbara Bray. For all rights, including performance rights, contact: Mercure de France, 26 rue de Condé, 75006 Paris, France.

p.87   extract from *Mary Barnes* by David Edgar, from *Barnes Plays 1*, Methuen Drama. Copyright © 1979, 1984 by David Edgar. Performance rights: Alan Brodie Representation Ltd, www.alanbrodie.com.

p.83   extract from *The Bitter Tears of Petra von Kant* by Rainer Werner Fassbinder, Amber Lane Press Ltd, 1984. Translation copyright © Anthony Vivas. Performance rights: Rosica Colin Ltd, 1 Clareville Grove Mews, London, SW7 5AH in the first instance.

p.107   extract from *The Open Couple* by Dario Fo, from *Fo Plays 2*, Methuen Drama. Translation copyright © 1985, 1990 Stuart Hood. Performance rights (English language [excluding North America]): The Rod Hall Agency Ltd, www.rodhallagency.com. All other performance rights: Flavia Tolnay, The Tolnay Agency, Italy, email: info@tolnayagency.it / www.tolnayagency.it/eng.

p.103   extract from *Don Juan, or The Love of Geometry* by Max Frisch, from Frisch Four Plays, Methuen Drama. Translation copyright © 1969 by Michael Bullock. Performance rights: please contact Methuen Drama in the first instance.

p.41   extract from *Camille* by Pam Gems (based on *La Dame aux Camélias* by Alexander Dumas [son]), from *Three Plays*, Penguin, 1985. Adaptation copyright © Pam Gems. Professional performance rights: Casarotto Ramsay & Associates Ltd, www.casarotto.uk.com in the first instance. Amateur performance rights: Samuel French Ltd, www.samuelfrench-london.co.uk.

p.74   extract from *The Maids* by Jean Genet, Faber & Faber Ltd.

Translation copyright © Bernard Frechtman. Performance rights: Éditions Gallimard, France, www.gallimard.fr. Performance rights in the UK: Rosica Colin Ltd, 1 Clareville Grove Mews, London, SW7 5AH in the first instance.

p.79   extract entitled *What Shall I Wear?* by Hermione Gingold. Copyright © The Estate of Hermione Gingold. Originally published in *The Years Between: Plays by Women on the London Stage 1900-1950*, edited by Fidelis Morgan, Virago Press, 1994.

p.143   extract from *Pour Lucrece* by Jean Giraudoux, translated as *Duel of Angels* by Christopher Fry, Methuen Drama, 1958. Translation copyright © 1958 Christopher Fry. Performance rights: contact Methuen Drama in the first instance.

p.64   extract from *K D Dufford hears K D Dufford ask K D Dufford how K D Dufford'll make K D Dufford* by David Halliwell, Faber & Faber Ltd, 1967. Copyright © David Halliwell.

p.67   extract from *Plenty* by David Hare, Faber & Faber Ltd, 1978. Copyright © David Hare. Performance rights: Casarotto Ramsay & Associates Ltd, www.casarotto.uk.com.

p.25   extract from *The Weavers* by Gerhart Hauptmann, Methuen Drama. Translation copyright © The Estate of Frank Marcus. Performance rights: Casarotto Ramsay & Associates Ltd, www.casarotto.uk.com.

p.44   extract from *The Bald Prima Donna* by Eugene Ionesco, from *Ionesco Plays Volume 1*, Calder Publications Ltd. Translation copyright © Donald Watson. Performance rights: Calder Publications Ltd, 51 The Cut, London, SE1 8LF in the first instance.

p.147   extract from *Ubu Rex* by Alfred Jarry from *The Ubu Plays*, Methuen Drama. Translation copyright © 1968 Cyril Connolly and Simon Watson Taylor. Professional and amateur performance rights: Rogers, Coleridge & White Ltd, www.rcwlitagency.com US & Canadian performance rights: The Dramatists Play Service Inc., USA, www.dramatists.com

p.71   extract from *Play with a Tiger* by Doris Lessing. Copyright © 1962 Doris Lessing. Used by kind permission of Jonathan Clowes Ltd, London, on behalf of Doris Lessing. Performance rights: Jonathan Clowes Ltd, Literary Agents, 10 Iron Bridge House, Bridge Approach, London, NW1 8BD.

p.124   extract from *Dona Rosita The Spinster* by Frederico García Lorca, from Lorca Plays: 1, Methuen Drama. Translation copyright © Gwynne Edwards. Professional performance rights: William

performance rights: The Peters, Fraser and Dunlop Group Ltd, www.pfd.co.uk. Amateur performance rights: Samuel French Ltd, www.samuelfrench-london.co.uk.

p.53   extract from *Saint's Day* by John Whiting. Originally published in *The Collected Plays of John Whiting* by Heinemann in 1969. Copyright © The Estate of John Whiting. Professional performance rights: The Peters, Fraser and Dunlop Group Ltd, www.pfd.co.uk.

p.121   extract from *A Woman of No Importance* by Oscar Wilde, from *Wilde Complete Plays*, Methuen Drama.

p.135   extract from *The Glass Menagerie* by Tennessee Williams, Methuen Drama. Copyright © 1945, renewed 1973 The University of the South, USA. Professional performance rights: Georges Borchardt, Inc., 136 East 57th Street, New York, NY 10022, USA. Amateur performance rights: Samuel French Ltd, www.samuelfrench-london.co.uk. US & Canadian performance rights: The Dramatists Play Service Inc., USA, www.dramatists.com

p.99   extract from *The Night of the Iguana* by Tennessee Williams, from *Cat on a Hot Tin Roof, The Milk Train Doesn't Stop Here Anymore and The Night of the Iguana*, Penguin Books, 2001. Copyright © The University of the South, USA. Professional performance rights: Georges Borchardt, Inc., 136 East 57th Street, New York, NY 10022, USA. Amateur performance rights: US & Canadian performance rights: The Dramatists Play Service Inc., USA, www.dramatists.com.